From Mainland to Maui

Awakening From "The American Dream"

By David J. Gross

All rights reserved.

ISBN: 0983847908
ISBN-13: 978-0-9838479-0-8

Copyright © 2012 Present Mind Publishing

Table of Contents

Preface i

PART ONE 5

1. From Mainland 5
2. To Maui 15
3. Life in Due Time 26
4. Making the Move 35
5. A Glimpse of Success 50
6. Buying "The American Dream" 67
7. Submitting to the Soul 79
8. The Pleasant Reality of Success Redefined 86

PART TWO 97

S. Stop Everything 97

T. Think About Your Past 128

O. Observe Your Environment 138

P. Plan With Purpose 165

PREFACE

Is this worth my time and energy? We often go through life assuming that what we're doing is worth it, but have we ever stopped to ask the question? What is success? The dictionary defines success as, "a favorable or desired outcome", or, "the attainment of wealth, position, honors, or the like." Years ago, and in some parts of the world today, merely surviving would be considered successful. To the hunter, a dead carcass equaled success. To the gatherer, a filled basket was the desired outcome; success! But today, in America, a country with plenty of food and water, how do we define success?

This is a book encouraging you to ask these questions. It's divided into two sections, both with this same goal in mind. The first section describes my journey of leaving Cincinnati, Ohio to move to the island of Maui. Part two outlines the mindset I needed to do so by grading success through personal goals, rather than money and status.

When I first moved to Hawaii with my girlfriend at the age of twenty, I had it all figured out. We would live on Maui for one year, become engaged, move back to the Mainland, get married, start profitable careers, buy a house, have kids, and live happily ever after. We would pursue what I believed to be "The American Dream", and we were on our way. We spent nearly one year on Maui working 25 hours a week and spent every day enjoying the beaches and exploring the island. We then became engaged, returned to the Mainland, purchased nice things, and began settling down in the city of Asheville, North Carolina; nestled in the Appalachian Mountains and just a six-hour drive from our family. Then I asked the question just like I had when I decided to drop out of college; "is this worth my irreplaceable time and effort?"

I've included my experiences as a form of credentials to show that what I'm saying is something I truly believe. I'm personally skeptical of taking advice and always want to ensure a statement is backed with action. There are too many financial advisors with no savings of their own and too many Ford salesmen who drive Toyotas. Telemarketers sell get-rich-quick programs, but if the programs worked and they truly believed them, why would they be telemarketing?!

I've included my story to establish how I've gained the mental perspective I have today. While there is humor and drama, stories of adventure and accounts of hardship, it's written to encourage you to pursue your dreams. I want you to consider what you're trying to accomplish with your time and effort so you may live in peace, knowing that the choices you make are precisely what you deem to be worthwhile. That being said, I am not as descriptive as if I were writing a full autobiography or novel for entertainment, so if it seems to move fast, it's intentional. While this section is presented first, either part can be read in whichever order you prefer.

Part two has four chapters using the acronym **S.T.O.P.** - **S**top Everything, **T**hink about Your Past, **O**bserve Your Environment, and **P**lan with Purpose. This is the method I've developed to create a personal definition of success in order to pursue something extraordinary. This approach examines how our influences (society, family, peers, etc.) have molded what we value and have consequently affected how we spend our time and effort. Have we considered what we want for our life or are we mindlessly doing what's expected of us? Are we carving our own path or are we blindly following the directions given by others?

From Mainland to Maui

As someone who has lived in the United States his whole life, I believe "The American Dream" is no longer defined as "that dream of a land in which life should be better and richer and fuller for every man, with opportunity for each according to ability or achievement", as first coined by James Truslow Adams in 1931. I believe it's more specific today. We're now deceived into believing that success is measured through money and status. When this came to be I'll leave for historians to study. I'm more interested in determining whether or not I want to accept this new definition as truth.

This book was not written to encourage you to move to Maui, but to find your own definition of paradise, then do whatever it takes to get there. As hundreds of thousands of students graduate from high school and college, millions of baby boomers retire, billions of people populate the planet, and we, as a country, are trillions of dollars in debt, it's time for something new. Join me in making the leap from Mainland to Maui and awakening from "The American Dream"!

PART ONE

1. FROM MAINLAND

I awake to the sound of birds chirping. Moseying my way into the kitchen for a fresh cup of Kona coffee I gaze out the window to view the spectacle; the marvelous sun rising behind mighty Haleakala, exposing the silhouette of the enormous volcano. There are no clouds caressing the ridged outline this early in the morning, only shades of the sky's light blue. I walk to the sliding glass door of my lanai for a glimpse of the massive Pacific Ocean. It resembles a gentle lake, with glassy and calm, navy-blue water. In the distance are the islands of Lana'i and Kaho'olawe, along with the mountains comprising West Maui. There are no sounds from cars, sirens, or people. All I hear is the quiet motor of my living room ceiling fan and the soothing serenade of Myna birds welcoming the day. Surrounding our cozy, two-bedroom condo are hundreds of plants and flowers filling the air with their fragrance. Sipping my hot beverage, I think about the day ahead. I have no stress or reason to feel anxiety.

Years ago, I felt guilty for having such a carefree life. It was a time when I believed that life couldn't be as good as I had it; a time when reality had surpassed my level of imagination. I used to be accustomed to a way of living where I couldn't see life for what it was; a time when everything felt like a dream, and to remain in that dream felt irresponsible and impossible. I still feel I'm dreaming, but it's okay now. Why did I once feel guilty?

This is the story of my experiences and observations that have led me to answer that question, along with others. The following pages describe my life and what I've learned by pursuing what I felt to be worth my time and energy. How did I get here? Where did it all begin?

It began with a youthful dream. I was thirteen years old when my mother took my brother and me on vacation to the island of Maui. My mom was divorced, hardworking, and frugal with her money. Having grown up in poverty, she had learned to stretch dollars wherever she could. Whether coupon clipping, buying the off-brand, or shopping at thrift stores, she was always able to save money. Through this penny pinching, she, my brother, and I were able to spend ten days on the white sandy beaches of Maui. This is where I first learned that you don't need much money to have extraordinary experiences.

We stayed in the beach town of Kihei (KEY-HAY), in a vacation condo rather than a hotel. It was cheaper than the resorts and we could cook our own meals instead of eating at pricey restaurants. Kihei was a small town surrounded by a multitude of beaches perfect for swimming, playing in the waves, and admiring the world beneath the surface in their crystalline waters. Every day my mom sunbathed while my younger brother and I body boarded, snorkeled, and played in the water. The total cost for our beach entertainment was twenty dollars for board rentals, plus the cost of sunscreen.

After a week of vacation, I was in love. Maui was the best place I'd been in my short life. One day, the three of us drove to Lahaina in West Maui, about thirty minutes from Kihei, to explore the coastal town and watch the sunset. As hundreds of tourists lined Front Street clinging to their cameras and hoping for a stunning shot of the setting sphere, it happened; my dream was birthed. I saw the ocean displaying another island in the distance and the sun moving into the horizon. I felt the soft breeze gently caressing my skin. I smelled the salty air from the water crashing along the rock wall where I sat, and in that moment, everything seemed perfect.

From Mainland to Maui

As the world of people surrounding me gazed through camera lenses, I saw the land with my naked eye. I saw the waves of the ocean dancing with the sunlight reflecting off the surface and the hues of a billion colors meshing into a picture replicated by no one but recreated by artists for centuries. I saw what was, and it didn't have a name. The other tourists didn't see the same thing I saw. They saw "Hawaii". They saw paradise. They saw what they had expected to see while looking at photos, books, and websites back home on the Mainland. What I saw, I saw alone.

It was obvious that Maui had better weather and more natural beauty than Ohio. I enjoyed it more than where I lived, and for me, at the age of thirteen, not spending most of my time in a preferred place didn't make sense. That night I told myself and my mom that one day I would move to Hawaii. I wasn't sure when the time would come, but at some point I would make the move. Our vacation ended a few days later and the idea of living on Maui was suppressed shortly thereafter.

The next several years disappeared in a flash, starting with my parents getting remarried. My mom's new husband had a house and job in Southern Maryland, so my brother and I moved with her from Cincinnati to the small, rural city of Leonardtown. A few months after leaving the only place I had ever known, I was homesick. I missed my friends and family in Cincinnati, so, at the age of fifteen, I returned and moved in with my dad and step-mom.

Back in my hometown I enrolled in public school and graduated with little effort. I walked the aisle with a 3.0 GPA having never read an entire book, passing tests by studying just minutes before they were given, copying homework, and never giving importance to education. I bid farewell to my high school years at a graduation party busted by the cops for underage drinking- I avoided arrest by fleeing through the woods while intoxicated.

A few weeks later I mindlessly enrolled at a branch of the University of Cincinnati located ten minutes from home. It seemed like an obvious choice and saved the expense of living on campus. I then needed to choose my major. I didn't know what career or job I wanted after college, but thinking back, I never really thought about life after college. In fact, I never really thought about life at all. I spent time that summer soul searching, trying to determine who I was to match with a job description. I spent hours online taking aptitude tests, hoping "the experts" would help me unveil a career that would fit who I was.

What classes would I prefer? What jobs are in high demand with good pay? What fits me as a person? What would fit my personality and what I value in life? What "career path" would be a good road to take?

After much deliberation, I settled on a business major. It seemed like a good choice; broad and with many opportunities. While not thrilled with my decision, I wasn't overly concerned. I had always heard, based on statistics, that I would change my major at least twice before graduating. Either way, the courses were all identical for the first two years, so I felt no pressure. It never made much sense to me, the same courses taken by nearly everyone, but it did give me peace of mind knowing I couldn't screw up my decision for at least two years.

The second issue needing attention while preparing for college was money. My family was middle class, leaning toward the lower side of middle, and my parents didn't have thousands of dollars set aside for my college education. The three of us (my mom, my dad, and I) all decided that we would each pay a third of the tuition and that I would remain living at home with my dad.

At the time I held a part-time job as a food runner for a chain Italian restaurant that was intended to cover my portion for college. Food-running had been my third job since starting my first when I was fifteen blending smoothies at a mall food court to pay for my first car. I continued working through high school to pay for gas, car insurance, fast food, and clothes, but now I needed money for tuition. Before I even stepped foot in a college classroom, I wrote a check for $1,500 to cover my portion for the first semester. This was the equivalent of two months' pay and the majority of what I had in the bank.

Before graduating from high school, I had fallen in love with the most wonderful girl named Miranda. She had researched several colleges but decided to stay in Cincinnati and attend the main campus of The University of Cincinnati just thirty minutes away. Although we didn't see each other at school, we worked at the same restaurant. She had started as a hostess and, upon reaching the age of 19 (legal age in Ohio for serving alcohol), we both began waiting tables.

My first day of college was quite similar to the first day of high school. The girls all wore new, brand-named clothes, and it was obvious the guys spent extra time styling their hair. Nervousness and excitement filled the hallways as students searched for the room numbers printed on their schedules. The freshmen sheepishly looked around for old high school classmates while the veteran sophomores mingled with their friends from the previous year. Entering the massive building, I wandered the hall with my forty pounds of required cellophane-wrapped textbooks strapped to my back before finding my first class; Accounting 101.

I dropped my thousand dollars' worth of printed materials on the floor and took a seat. The professor stood at the front of the class and told us to look around the room, estimating that nearly 50% of us wouldn't be there in a month. He projected that half of the class would either drop out or flunk. I had always done well in school without much effort, so I sat with my arms crossed and viewed this "greeting" as a freshman scare tactic. I quickly learned that I wasn't the genius I thought I was but had simply graduated from a school with low standards.

Within my first three weeks I dropped my accounting and history classes. Dropping these classes freed some time, but not much, and I couldn't find enough hours in the day to do everything I wanted. Back in high school I had plenty of time to spend with Miranda and my friends, but not here. All of my time was spent studying or working and there were simply not enough hours in the day to get good grades, spend time with friends, sleep eight hours, and work to pay for college. It wasn't possible.

What can I change? Should I get less sleep? Should I not have friends? Is college even worth it? Do I have other options? If so, what are they?

In considering options outside of college I looked at the full-time waiters and waitresses I worked with. One had a master's degree in English who, when applying for a "real" job, was told she was either over-qualified or under-experienced. She had been waiting tables for years while career hunting. One waiter was a retired drug dealer who, after many years of not being caught, decided to no longer take the risk. He had made hundreds of thousands of dollars selling drugs and had nothing to show for it but a stiff walk and lingering addiction. An older woman worked to supplement her husband's income and saved most of her tips to go toward their yearly vacation. Every winter near the peak of whale season, she and her husband would spend ten days on Maui. She loved Maui, and even carried a picture of a breaching Humpback Whale glued to the front of her dupe pad.

Most of the "career servers" seemed miserable and viewed their lives as failures for holding such lowly positions in society. They'd walk around from table to table with cheesy smiles and high-pitched voices while secretly feeling victimized and dissatisfied with life. They would artificially laugh with strangers, hoping for a better tip, and then cuss them out in the kitchen. Even the managers who were paid more and received full medical and retirement benefits seemed unhappy.

From Mainland to Maui

One weekday morning with class scheduled for 8:30 A.M., my alarm woke me up to reveal the dismal weather I'd soon be forced to endure. It was cold and wet; not snowing or raining, just a mix of the two that quickly turns into gray slush. Dragging myself out of bed and throwing on some clothes, I sluggishly went to my teal, '92 hatchback. Cold air blew on my face as I started the car and didn't warm up the entire drive to campus. Irritable and nearly frostbitten, I parked my car and started my hike to the college building. When I finally got to my psychology class, I sat down, took off my hat and gloves, and then spent the next hour struggling to stay awake through an outdated, low-budget film about neurons.

With twenty minutes until my next class, "Business 101", I stepped outside to smoke a cigarette. I stood by myself in the designated smoking area hugging a wall for protection from the arctic wind. I was standing in the midst of America's future; my classmates, bundled in their new brand-named coats and designer jeans. I saw a clique talking about last night's party and planning for the next. I saw a group of outcasts trying to blend in with the crowd. Some students appeared to be enjoying themselves, laughing and conversing, while others kept awkwardly silent. To me, they all looked gray and lifeless. Not only did the people look washed out, but everything else did as well. The sky was gray, the ground was gray, and everything in between appeared as various shades of gray. Even the noise sounded dull and muffled, contributing to the tasteless and stale environment.

As I continued sucking my filtered roll of cheap tobacco, I viewed myself from an outsider's perspective. I saw what I was wearing and who and what surrounded me. I examined how I felt, what I smelled, and the way my current situation was impacting my thoughts. Then, standing there chattering my teeth in between pulls, I faced reality.

David J. Gross

I'm majoring in business and have no idea why or what that even means. I sadly attend classes where I'm not having fun and not learning anything I feel of value. When I'm not in class I see dull shades of gray while freezing my butt off, and on top of all that, I'm waiting tables to pay for it!

Finishing my cigarette and contemplating these observations, I recalled my high school guidance counselors, teachers, and the many websites I had visited. I thought of the conversations with my coworkers and the many statistics I had read. All of these sources, sources older and smarter than me, all repeated the same thing. They said that in order to have a good job and be successful, you need to have a college education and four-year degree.

All of these people must be right, but am I really supposed to believe I need to go through the misery of college for nothing more than a possible "good" job in the future? What's their definition of good? If I suffer through four years of misery, will it be worth the reward?

Call me stubborn, naïve, or stupid, but, to me, it didn't make sense. I couldn't buy into the belief that in order to be happy I needed to spend time and money on a degree. Sadly, I was doing something I didn't want to do and had no answer for why I was doing it. I also knew attending college was not a matter of life or death. I could survive without a degree. I wasn't happy with what I was doing and couldn't convince myself it was worth it, so I left.

Walking back to the car, I was no longer bothered by my numb feet and goose-bumped skin. I was skipping class and didn't know where I would go or what I would do but realized that I was putting a great deal of time and effort into something I didn't enjoy. Life wasn't working for me, I was working for life, and it was a life of blindly pursuing what I'd been told was ideal. On my way to the parking lot, my mind raced with uncertainties, questions, fears and anxieties about what my life would be like if I didn't return. But ultimately, it didn't matter, for I was leaving what I knew I didn't want.

I didn't know all of my options, but, had I stayed, I never would have had the time to search for them. That night I decided to finish the classes for which I had already paid and then leave college at the end of the semester. Several weeks later I passed Business 101 with an A, and both English and Psychology with B's.

I then started working full-time while still living with my dad and step-mom. Miranda, with whom I was now getting very close, decided to also leave college and work full-time. Life after dropping out wasn't bad. In fact, it was pretty good. I had food to eat, my own room at home, plenty of time with my friends, dates with Miranda, and money. I frequented restaurants, went to movies, attended parties, and had no worries.

Unfortunately, this life of leisure didn't last long. The startling news came when my dad informed me that he and his wife would be getting divorced. He would be the one leaving the house, and with me as a nineteen-year-old with a full-time job, I had no reason to not get my own place. It was time for me to be on my own; paying my own rent, buying my own food, and covering my own living expenses.

Miranda was living with her mom at the time. Her mother, Lori, was recently divorced and still getting acquainted with apartment life when Miranda and I decided to get an apartment of our own. After a week of looking, we signed a one-year lease on a one-bedroom unit in an older complex without any frills; but we loved it. We had little money, hand-me-down furniture, and only a few belongings, but made the small apartment a great first home.

We loved each other and enjoyed the freedoms of being on our own, despite the new expenses it incurred. However, while we were proud of ourselves and grateful for the home we'd established, we wanted something different. We wanted something better. We couldn't see the gray skies continuously blanketing the city without getting headaches, and the time we spent sitting in traffic jams was wasted, spent only looking forward to the destination to which we were traveling. Billboards lined every highway. Sleet, snow, rain, hot, cold, grumpy, and crowded was how we viewed southwest Ohio. We perceived the area as dull and its people as bitter complainers who were never content about anything.

I want something different, but what are the options? When and where have I been most happy? When and where did I feel alive and excited about life? Maui

2. TO MAUI

It was another overcast day in the suburbs of Cincinnati, Ohio when I presented the idea to Miranda.

"Why don't we move to Hawaii," I said half-jokingly.

She laughed, "Ha! I know you're not serious."

"Why not," I responded. "What if we saved up and moved there for just a year. One year in Hawaii and then move back to settle down. We're nineteen; we don't need to worry about careers and houses and kids right now. What's the worst-case scenario?"

Knowing she wouldn't go for it, I mainly asked just wanting to see how my girlfriend of two years would react to such an outrageous proposal. She had been raised in the Midwest and was not well traveled; taking a Caribbean cruise as a child and once visiting her aunt in Colorado, but that was it. She could barely fathom a vacation to Hawaii, let alone moving there.

Over the next several weeks we began noticing how many times the words and images of Hawaii appeared in daily life. Advertisements, television shows, and radio stations capitalized on the dreamy paradise, and the more times it was mentioned, the more I reminisced.

I described my time on Maui to Miranda, "You don't understand babe. Everyday is perfect in Hawaii! The relaxed attitude is felt from every person and in every place. The sun's hot, but the heat is always countered by the cool breeze of the trades."

"Then let's just move there already," Miranda said. "I'm tired of hearing about it and it's obviously what you want. Let's go!"

I don't know why she said it. Maybe she was tired of hearing me complain about Cincinnati, or maybe she was testing to see if I was serious. A lump formed in the back of my throat as I envisioned selling everything we owned and moving thousands of miles away to one of the most isolated places in the world.

I responded, "OK! Then let's do it. But Miranda, have you thought this through? Do you really want to move? You do understand how far away Hawaii is, don't you? We would have to sell everything, leave our apartment, and not see our families for the entire year we lived there. Are you serious?"

"Why not," she responded as if she was trying to show me up. "We don't have that much stuff, and it's only a year. If we get out there and it doesn't work out, we can always come back. Let's do it, seriously."

I took a deep breath, feeling as though she was now the one trying to convince me. Miranda didn't care much for Cincinnati, and while she had never been to Hawaii, she assumed it would be better than the Midwest. So, with the goal of moving, we started planning.

We looked into the different areas of all the islands before deciding on where I had vacationed; Kihei, Maui. We would sell most of our things, store some at my dad's house, and pack nothing other than clothes. We planned to view the year on Maui as a break from the real world; like an extended vacation where we just happened to work. But first, we needed money, and after much research figured we needed $10,000: $2,000 for one-way tickets, $1,000 for temporary lodging,

$3,000 for rent, $2,000 for a cheap older car, and another $2,000 for emergencies.

An hourly wage of $2.13 plus tips made $10,000 look like a mountain of money. We could have been discouraged and viewed our goal as impossible, but we didn't. In fact, coming up with a realistic financial goal to work toward did just the opposite. With knowing we needed ten thousand dollars before we left, we were able to see our destination as tangible. We didn't just say we want to move to Hawaii and need a lot of money to do it; that would have kept the dream a fantasy.

"What are we going to do when we get there?" Miranda asked.

"Well, we can get jobs waiting tables. But I have an idea. There's an Outback Steakhouse in Kihei," I proudly said having done some research, "and if we get a job at an Outback here, maybe we could transfer. Even if we couldn't, we'd have a better chance of getting hired at the one in Kihei having already worked at an Outback here."

Miranda agreed it would be worth a shot, so we applied at the nearest Outback location that was hiring. Without revealing our primary reason for wanting the job, we were both hired as servers and quit our old jobs. Wanting to make great first impressions to better our chances of transferring, we memorized the menu and every ingredient verbatim. We stood out. Most of the other servers were either college students who didn't take the job seriously or people working for extra holiday cash. Few actually worked there full-time, and the ones that did just went through the motions with little enthusiasm. So while we didn't have much competition, we strived to be two of the best.

Hours of online research at home filled every day while preparing for the move. Where would we live? What other jobs are available if we can't work at Outback? How will we get around? I wanted to eliminate as many uncertainties as I could before boarding the plane, and with every bit of information I read, not only did my worries exit my thoughts, but my dream transformed into more of a reality.

The Hawaiian Islands were 4,369 miles from where we lived, making them feel almost imaginary. One night after a slow, unprofitable shift at work, I decided to call the Outback in Kihei to see how busy they were.

A young girl answered the phone, "Aloha, Outback Steakhouse, how may I help you?"

I spoke nervously, "Umm, hi. I was just wondering if you were on a wait and how long the wait was."

"It's currently about thirty minutes, but it's starting to slow down."

"OK, thank you!"

Up until this point my planning had been limited to maps, books, articles, and pictures, but not anymore. Now I had personally interacted with someone who was living and working on Maui. Speaking to the hostess of the Kihei Outback made the restaurant come alive in my living room. While I could only see Maui through pictures and classified ads for jobs and places to live, in my thirty second phone call I touched the island. It helped silence everyone and everything that created the image of Hawaii as a vacationer's paradise to now view it as a place where people worked, ran errands, and paid bills. It was a fantasy to millions, but home to a few.

We wanted to join those who called Maui home for just a year to get the experience and wanted to get there as quickly as possible. Knowing my mom excelled at saving money, we asked for her help in setting up a budget. It was tricky with our pay structure, as our tips and hours changed daily, so she showed us what she called, "the envelope system". We would keep all our tips in one envelope then distribute the funds every week for rent, food, etc. We kept expenses to a minimum so all the money left over could go toward moving.

Life at home was basic. We'd wake up, sit around the house for a while, go to work, get home, eat dinner, watch a movie, and then go to bed. Grocery store visits were very strict, budgeting around $50 a week. This didn't give funds for steaks and bottles of wine, so we drank tap water and ate deli sandwiches or cans of soup for lunch. For dinner, we'd make chicken on a George Foreman Grill served with instant mashed potatoes and canned corn. We frequently ate this meal by candle light. Dinner cost three dollars for us both; the romantic candle-lit dinner conversations were free.

For entertainment, with the exception of going out to eat once a week, we watched TV and movies. We didn't love movies, but in Cincinnati it's the norm to sit on the couch and watch a screen. We went without cable TV and used "rabbit ears" for a while, but eventually the static led us to order basic cable- not the basic cable with 70 something channels, just local ones in clear picture for ten bucks a month. We didn't spend much time flipping through five channels, so we mainly watched movies borrowed from the library. They were completely free, so we'd pick up around five each visit.

It wasn't always easy, and in the year of working and saving, we lived poor; relative to our environment of course. One day as I was shopping for work clothes at Wal-Mart, I overheard a woman yelling on her cell phone, "Listen, they're just like Dockers! Why do they need to be that brand? I'm getting these for you anyway, and if you don't like 'em I'll take 'em back!"

I continued rummaging through the overfilled racks of shirts as she hung up her phone in frustration. Knowing I heard her conversation, she looked at me to explain, "It's my son. For some reason he will only wear khaki pants that are Dockers brand. I don't understand!"

"Yeah," I responded. "I used to think that way too until I started supporting myself. Now a ten-dollar pair of pants doesn't look so bad."

The woman smiled. I no longer cared about things like brand named clothes or having the newest electronics. I knew that every dollar I spent equaled that much longer until I made it to Maui.

A few months later, after I had eaten everything on Outback's menu at least once, I was unsatisfied. Waiting tables at Outback Steakhouse wasn't terrible, but it lacked formality. Slinging burgers, sirloins, and Cokes to people making sure they get their money's worth on a $1.65 soda with free refills wasn't my style; not bad, just not my preference. We had a nice idea of transferring, but I wasn't going to sacrifice my happiness in the present for a possible future reward, so I started looking for another place to work.

Days later I heard there was a new restaurant opening near our apartment of the Italian chain I had previously worked, so I left Outback for my old restaurant in a new and different location. Miranda also transferred stores and moved to an Outback closer to home. We both worked five days a week but arranged to have the same two days off.

To those we spoke with in Cincinnati, moving to Maui was unrealistic. In some areas of the country it's common to move, but the Midwest is not one of these areas. We were surrounded by suburban families who rarely traveled and lived within systematic routines and schedules. It seemed that everyone had a concern or negative outlook toward our plan of moving to Hawaii, and after a while, we stopped talking about it altogether.

From Mainland to Maui

"I couldn't believe this guy, another server," Miranda said getting home from work. "I told him where we were moving and he said, 'You're not moving to Maui. My parents have a timeshare there.'"

"What do his parents owning a timeshare have anything to do with us moving?" I asked.

"I don't know! I think his parents are rich, so he's thinking that if they can only afford to be there one week every year then we certainly can't afford to be there all year round. He didn't know what he was talking about and he sounded like an idiot!"

"Ha-ha," I couldn't take him too seriously. "Miranda, nobody wants to believe that we or anyone else can live in Hawaii. They'd rather just complain and view the idea as impossible. Get his address and we'll send him a postcard when we get there!"

Every person who viewed us as naïve or showed pessimism just gave us more motivation to move. Most people's argument against living in Hawaii was the expense. Hawaii was statistically the most expensive state in the nation, and Maui was the most expensive island in the state. Cincinnati, on the other hand, is one of the cheapest cities in the country to live. But it didn't matter, because I had done the research and knew we could afford the cost of living. I had looked online for rentals, and while I didn't find much in the line of apartments, Hawaii had many ohanas (mother-in-law suites) for rent. With real estate and rent being extremely pricey, nearly every house either had an attached or detached ohana. Some came furnished, while others did not. They came in all shapes, sizes, and terms, but I came to find that many were relatively affordable. I saw a few that were around $1,200 a month, making it realistic to live on Maui as long as we could make the same amount of money as we already did. Twelve hundred dollars can pay for the mortgage for a decent house in Cincinnati, so I can see where people thought we were insane for wanting to pay the same amount to rent a couple rooms in someone else's house. But to us ohanas seemed perfect. They made it possible to move to Hawaii, even if our neighbors in Cincinnati didn't believe us.

"Miranda, we've been staying within our budget and soon we'll have met our goal," I said while beginning to think about the logistics of the move.

"Well, I have a question," Miranda said. "How will we get around once we get there? We won't have a car right away and we're too young to rent one. Do you have any thoughts?"

"Well, there is a bus service, but it's new and the routes are limited. We could just get taxis for a few days until we bought a car."

"Dave, we'll go broke! Taxis are so expensive."

"That's true," I was discouraged. "Well here's an idea. I don't know if she'll go for it or not, but what if my mom joined us? She wouldn't need to be there for long, only until we bought a car, and we could pay for the rental car and her lodging."

"It's worth a shot. Ask her and see what she says."

My mom took a few days to answer once I asked but said she would help. She declined our offer to pay but demanded that we needed to find a car and place to live by the time she left. She didn't want to stay longer than planned and wouldn't feel right leaving us homeless and without transportation. Just a few weeks after she agreed to join, we reached our financial goal.

In looking for one-way plane tickets to Maui, I felt ripped off. They were nearly the same price as roundtrip, and I didn't understand why! At work I brought up the situation to some of my co-workers.

From Mainland to Maui

"Well, we have enough money to move, but flights are so expensive! And there's barely any price difference between round trip and one-way. It's ridiculous! I'm almost tempted to buy round-trip and then see if I can return it once we're there."

One of the servers who was listening responded, "My step-dad works for an airline and gets us free flights, so I wouldn't know. Maybe he can get you and Miranda a discount or something. Maybe even free flights! He gets a certain number every year and I can ask him if he has any extras."

"That would be awesome! Anything he could do for us would be greatly appreciated!"

The following week I received a call from the girl's step-dad whom I had never met, "Hello, is this David?"

I answered, "Yes."

"David, I'm Lauren's dad. She said you were moving to Maui and were looking for plane tickets?"

My heart began racing as I pressed the phone closer to my ear, "Yes! How are you?"

"I'm fine. Anyway, I could probably get you some buddy passes if you have a date in mind you'd like to go. You'd just need to pay the taxes which probably won't be more than a couple hundred bucks."

I couldn't believe it as I stuttered, "Really? Well are you sure? I...I...I mean...that would be great if you could, but..."

"No, it's not a problem. I get around a dozen a year and usually have to throw some away. It's flying standby, but there are usually extra seats."

Hanging up the phone, I was ecstatic. The flights that would have cost us nearly two thousand dollars ending up costing less than $150! We picked our dates, and with standby tickets in hand, Miranda went to work. The day had come to tell her boss she was moving to Maui and wanted to transfer.

"Alright, wish me luck," Miranda told me as she was leaving.

I could tell she was nervous, but coming home was a different story.

"Well, how'd it go?" I asked as Miranda opened the door to our apartment.

"You're not going to believe this," she said smiling and laughing as she spoke. "I waited until the end of night to tell him, and then at the end of the night," she paused to reminisce in disbelief, "I told him where we were moving, and he was thrilled for us! He said he had lived on Kauai years ago until his house burnt down in a fire and told me that he would make the Kihei Outback feel like fools if they wouldn't accept his best employee! He told me I would most likely have a job as soon as we land!"

"That's awesome babe! See, you were worried for no reason. Now you just have to tell your dad."

While Miranda had already told her mom we were moving, she had procrastinated in telling her dad. She was extremely anxious about breaking the news, but after letting him know we would only be there a year and had money saved, he was supportive. He even threw us a Hawaiian-themed going away party the week before we left!

The year of working to make our move was nearing its end. We gave notice to our apartment manager by letting her know we'd be leaving once our lease expired. We were really doing it, and in our first year of being on our own we'd saved over ten thousand dollars, become closer in our relationship, and found success by working toward a valued goal. Everything had gone wonderfully, and the only thing left to do was to say our goodbyes; including one tragic, final farewell that would change everything

3. LIFE IN DUE TIME

Less than a week before we were scheduled to fly to Maui, Miranda and I spent an evening with Lori, Miranda's mom, Lori's boyfriend, and one of Miranda's brothers. Before going out to eat, the five of us toured Lori's newly purchased condo she was preparing to move into. It was the first time we had seen it, and Lori was thrilled to show it off. The walls were freshly painted with light browns and dark greens, and a new living room set had recently been delivered.

As Lori led us through her brand-new condo, you could see her mind racing with decorating ideas. She paced the dining area that flowed into the living room, "I'm thinking of putting a little dinette set here and then getting some outdoor carpet to go on the patio for my new puppy. It's too bad you guys won't get a chance to see it before you move. I'll have to send pictures."

Lori was also happy for us moving, although you could tell the idea of her only daughter living over 4,000 miles away naturally made her nervous. But she didn't talk about it, and only discussed how excited she was for us. After leaving her condo, she treated us to her favorite Mexican restaurant, and after margaritas and enchiladas, we all caravanned to Miranda's oldest brother's apartment. With it being our final week in Cincinnati, we wanted to see our families as much as we could.

A couple hours later we hugged everyone goodbye and started our forty-five-minute drive back home in the rain with lightning blanketing the sky. We had planned that same night to meet with some friends from work who had arranged a small get together for Miranda and me. Dressed and ready to walk out the door, we received a phone call from Lori's boyfriend. He hurriedly told Miranda that her mother was heading to the hospital in an ambulance. Without much detail, he said it was important we came back to see her.

Getting off the phone, Miranda was confused and frustrated. We had just drove forty miles home in the rain and were getting ready to go to a party. It would be the last chance we'd get to see our friends from work and Miranda believed everything was fine with her mom. She didn't see how we were needed at the hospital and questioned how ill her mother really was. So, she asked me to call Lori's boyfriend to see how crucial it was that we came.

I went in the other room and called him back, "Hi. Miranda wanted me to see how important it was that we come down. We were getting ready…"

"It's very important," he said, voice quavering as he spoke. "Drive safe but get here as soon as you can. You guys need to be here."

He didn't need to say anymore. Although I didn't want to believe it, I already knew what had happened; I knew Lori had died.

"We'll be there as soon as possible," I said quickly hanging up the phone.

Driving back to Northern Kentucky I tried convincing myself that my instincts were wrong. Miranda sat in the passenger side, half concerned and half irritated, positive that her mom was perfectly fine. When we were just a few miles away from the hospital I gave up trying to be optimistic about Lori's condition and submitted to my instinctive knowledge of the truth. I knew that when we got to the hospital

Miranda would not find her mother alive, and I didn't have a clue of what to do. What could I do? I'd never had someone that close to me die, nor could I fathom the horror of encountering something so nightmarish.

Just before arriving at the ER, I tried getting Miranda to consider the worst, hoping to cut down on her inevitable shock, "Miranda, I'm sure everything's fine, but no matter what, everything will be okay. I'm here for you. Your dad, your brothers, and I all love you very much."

"Dave, everything's fine," Miranda confidently told me. "My mom isn't too healthy and gets sick all the time. We'll go in, visit with her for a little while and then leave. She's probably going to feel silly that we drove back to see her."

Arriving at the hospital, we walked to the counter asking where Lori had been taken. Miranda went to the registration desk of the ER, "Hi, we're here to see Lori, I'm her daughter."

The receptionist looked up, looked at Miranda, and then looked at me, "Some of your family is already here. If you'll just wait inside that room," she said pointing to a door.

We entered the small private waiting room and saw one of Miranda's brothers sitting with his girlfriend. He looked up from one of the two loveseats that filled the room with bloodshot eyes. Unable to speak, he prompted his girlfriend to inform us of the news.

"She didn't make it," his girlfriend said quietly.

Lori had suffered a fatal heart attack in the bathroom of her apartment just hours after saying goodbye to her two sons and only daughter; just hours after a blended strawberry margarita at her favorite Mexican restaurant, and just hours after giving us a tour of her new condo she'd never have a chance to enjoy.

I helplessly held Miranda as she wept and cried and screamed, overpowering the roar of thunder that continued outside. The entire hospital must have heard her wailing. Seconds later, Miranda jumped up and ran to the bathroom and got sick while I sat in disbelief and bewilderment. I couldn't believe it was possible, and even asked myself if I was dreaming. Many thoughts and emotions raced through my head while I stared into space. I thought about what I could do for Miranda, understanding my presence and affection were all I could give. I would do all I could for my girlfriend, who at the age of twenty, had just lost her mother to a sudden and unexpected heart attack. She was my first concern, but what about moving?

The dream that was Maui had lost all importance as I began pondering the many outcomes of what could potentially result:

What are we going to do? We have flights to leave in a few days and are scheduled to empty our apartment in the morning! Would we still move? How could we?! Would we stay in Cincinnati for a week, a month, or a year until everything was sorted out? Should we cancel or postpone our plans of moving to Maui and look for another apartment in Cincinnati? Maybe we should forget about Maui altogether.

Miranda returned from the bathroom only to leave again for the chapel of the hospital to be alone and pray. With Miranda in the chapel, her brother in silent shock, and the rest of her family on the way to the hospital, I decided to call my parents. I first called my mom who was still planning to leave for Maui with us in less than a week. It was around ten o'clock at night and she had already turned her phone off, so I called my dad. He was planning to meet us at our apartment in the morning to help us move, and with the leasing office expecting us to leave, that would remain unchanged.

Miranda returned from the chapel to meet the rest of her family who were standing outside discussing funeral arrangements. Lori would be buried in Iowa near the town in which she had been raised. We didn't stay much longer and drove back to our apartment for the last night in our first home. Opening the door, we wandered past the boxes that covered our living room floor and collapsed in bed.

Morning quickly came, bringing with it an overwhelming dose of reality. I woke up first, reliving the surreal events that had taken place just hours before. Miranda woke up shortly thereafter, and even before getting out of bed was struck with the realization that her mom was gone. For the rest of the day Miranda would only take breaks from crying to stare lifelessly in disbelief.

My dad showed up with the truck around nine o'clock to haul our belongings to his house to be stored or sold. Miranda and I were leaving our apartment; that was certain. Where we were moving, what we'd be doing, how we'd be living and the many other questions needing answered filled my mind. In the meantime, we would stay with my dad.

I would have loved to talk with Miranda about how she was feeling and what she was thinking but knew she was in no condition. So my dad and I began loading the U-haul while Miranda stayed in our bedroom. She laid on our full size mattress and box spring my dad had bought me when I was in high school. We never bothered getting a frame, and despite me being 6'3" tall, having the small mattress and box spring on the floor was satisfactory. While I would have preferred sleeping in a bed big enough that my feet didn't hang over the edge, buying anything more would have only prolonged us reaching our goal.

From Mainland to Maui

Upon lugging the last box from our apartment and returning the keys to the office manager, I began thinking about our current homeless state. Then I recapped the year. We had planned, saved, prepared and worked hard with great discipline. We spent very little on food, slept on an uncomfortable mattress, borrowed movies from the library for entertainment and had to adjust the volume on our television every time the heat kicked on to overcome the noise from the furnace. We worked hard and saved every dollar we could in order to move. But was moving the right thing to do now that Miranda's mom had just passed away?

I was frustrated and didn't know what to do, but it wasn't about me. The choice to move to Maui or stay in Cincinnati centered on my girlfriend whom I dearly loved unexpectedly losing her mother at such a young age. The question I needed to answer wasn't about moving, but about how I could be as supportive as possible. I answered that question by leaving the decision of where we would live entirely to Miranda. I loved her and would support her choice no matter what.

We both understood the position we were in. We had quit our jobs, didn't have a place to call home, had four suitcases of personal belongings, $10,000 in the bank, two standby tickets to Maui, and Lori's funeral to attend. Whether we stayed in Cincinnati or went to Maui, we would still need jobs and a place to live. We had nothing to keep us from moving, and Miranda was promised a job at the Outback in Kihei. On the other hand, her mom had just passed away, and to go start a new life in a foreign city seemed incomprehensible. The thought of moving to a place far away from family where we wouldn't know anyone was difficult to begin with, but to do it now seemed unimaginable.

I presumed Miranda's desire to move was gone. To go a year later was a faint hope in my mind as I waited for her to decide what we would do. After some thought and prayer, she surprised me by saying, "I think we should still move. If we stay here, there's nothing I can do to make it better. If anything, staying here would probably just make me miss her more. This whole city will never feel the same without her."

I listened patiently before asking, "Miranda, are you sure you want to do this?"

"I'm sure. It'll probably be good to get away. If I stay here I'll just think about her all the time. After the funeral we'll leave."

So it was settled; immediately following the funeral we'd fly to Maui.

As Miranda's family began making arrangements, I revised our trip. I first needed to tell my mom we were still coming, only a few days later than initially planned. The second thing to do was change our flights. Upon reaching the airline's "customer service representative", I explained the situation.

"Hi, I was hoping to change our flights scheduled for this Tuesday. There's been a death in the family."

The woman on the other line snapped back, "What's the relation of the deceased?"

"It's my girlfriend. Her mom just died."

"So, the person isn't related to you?"

I couldn't believe the lack of sympathy, "Well, no, but the other passenger is my girlfriend."

"What's your girlfriend's mother's name? When did she die? When is the funeral? What's the name of the funeral home?"

From Mainland to Maui

After answering what felt like a polygraph test, I was finally able to change the flights. The change didn't cost us any extra, and we actually received a small reimbursement for the price difference.

After scrambling to change what had been planned for months, our last days on the Mainland would consist of riding with Miranda's dad to the funeral in Iowa, visiting with Miranda's extended family who I had never met, saying our goodbyes at the funeral, and then bidding farewell to the rest of the family. After making the trip and spending a day with Miranda's uncles, aunts, cousins and grandparents, we attended the funeral. At the wake, after everyone's tears had dried and all the food was gone, we said goodbye. It was a long and emotional day, and the next day would feel even longer.

We spent the night at a family member's house and awoke six hours later before crawling into the rental van and heading to the airport. Once at the airport, we said goodbye to her father and brothers who were dropping us off, checked our bags, and walked through the sleepy terminal to our gate. It was 8:00 a.m. in Iowa, marking the beginning of our sixteen-hour trip.

We were moving; only without a truck, without boxes, without a couch and without a bed. We were moving. This was the biggest change Miranda and I had made in our twenty years of life on Earth. We had four suitcases of clothes, a couple books, one tennis racket, Lori's old digital camera, and a laptop computer.

We should have been excited, full of life and filled with wonder. We should have been thrilled at the thought of finally seeing the day we had dreamt about for the entire year. We should have had pride, a sense of completion and clinched success. But instead, we felt weak, tired, and sick. The past five days had rushed by, leaving us drained of all physical, mental, and emotional energy.

David J. Gross

It's interesting how life works sometimes. We had spent over a year working and saving money. We had both spent countless hours learning and planning as much as we could to avoid any mishaps. Throughout the year, I had envisioned our families eating a big dinner together on the night before our departure. I pictured us walking down the airport terminal smiling and waving as our loved ones waved back. But sitting in the terminal of the Cedar Rapids airport, struggling to stay awake, I learned a lesson I believe everyone learns at some point in their life: No matter how planned and prepared you can be, nothing is for certain and nothing lasts forever.

DING! "Now boarding through gate five is non-stop service to Los Angeles. All standby passengers are clear. Please watch your step getting on board.

From Mainland to Maui

4. MAKING THE MOVE

Our flight to L.A. made Miranda sick, and added to my anxiety about flying standby with not being assigned a seat until minutes before departure. With a limited number of flights to Maui, it was possible for us to be stranded in L.A. for an indefinite period. I was just hoping for a slow day at the airport, but when we reached the gate, I saw hundreds of people waiting to board.

The television monitor displayed the standby list of ten names. As ticketed passengers started boarding, the first two names cleared, leaving us next in line. We nervously waited as the plane filled, and then our names appeared, assigning us seats 4A and 4B. Not only would we get on the flight, but we would be flying first class. The flights for which we had paid $75 each would have cost around $3,000 had we paid regular fare.

Miranda fell asleep before the plane even moved while I evaluated whether I was awake or still dreaming. Leaning back in the cozy leather recliner and declining a glass of Chardonnay, I reflected on the past week. I thought of the last time I saw Miranda's mother on the "Good Friday" before Easter when she died. I recalled moving out of our apartment the morning after, rearranging our plans, and saying goodbye to my family in Cincinnati before the eight-hour drive to Waterloo, Iowa. My blurred memory relived meeting Miranda's large extended family for the first time, ordering flowers for the visitation, the open-casket funeral service, shaking hands with Miranda's father at the airport while promising to take care of his only daughter, our flight to Los Angeles and the anxiety of flying standby. The longest and most emotional week of my life had ended.

Miranda slept nearly the entire flight and awoke shortly before we landed. I remained awake, and all I could think of was ending the six hour flight. It was just getting dark when the island first appeared on the horizon, barely showing an outline of where the land met the water. Miranda pressed her face against the window looking out with a childlike curiosity and anticipation. I should have been just as excited, but I wasn't. With the courage to leave college, the discipline to save money, and the ambition to make the move, I should have been thrilled. I should have been ecstatic that my hard work was finally going to pay off, but instead, I was petrified.

What are we doing?! What have I done by bringing this girl here? Are we nuts?! This is crazy!

The city lights became brighter as the plane approached the runway while I sat in fear, blocking any positive thought that crossed my mind. Fear stopped me from remembering my research of how financially realistic it was to live on Maui. I deprived myself of joy and thought only about everything we had to do. We needed to buy a car. We needed to find a place to live. I needed to get a job. My mind continued racing with concerns...

What if our car breaks down right after we buy it? What if nobody will rent to us because we're so young? What if I can't find a job? What if we fail to cover our living expenses? What if...what if...what if...?

I viewed these needs (job, car, place to live) as mandatory, feeling as though we could die without them. Had I been calm in understanding these "needs" weren't needs at all, I could have experienced what should have been an incredible moment. Had I used logic over emotion, I would have perceived nothing to lose and everything to gain.

While my mind was overwhelmed with horrific scenarios for our future, Miranda sat quietly. Her mom had just died. She had lost her best friend, Mother, caretaker, and guardian. How meaningless are things like money and occupations just a day after the funeral? How could she fear when death was no longer an illusion, but a reality?

Had you seen me, you would have thought I'd flown to Maui on orders to be executed. Nothing I did could mask the anxiety tensing my face and body. However, when I stepped out of the gangway my feelings immediately changed. I was comforted by the soothing warm breeze of the open air terminal. The air smelled sweet, scented by hundreds of flowers lining the terminal's walkway. There were plenty of people talking and rolling their bags across the cement floor, yet everything seemed quiet. It wasn't like California, Iowa, Ohio, or any other place I knew. It felt calm. The streets, airports, malls, and sidewalks on the Mainland buzzed with energy; hurried, noisy and impersonal. But this was different, and walking to the baggage claim of the Kahului Airport, I didn't have a negative thought or ounce of anxiety. Just the opposite from onboard the airplane, my only thought was how pleasant the temperature felt and how fresh the air smelled. It was heavenly.

My mother was already waiting by the baggage claim with two purple Orchid leis. "It's so good to see you both," she said hugging us while fighting back tears of sympathy for Miranda.

It was dark by the time we left the airport, giving the slow island an even more mellowed vibe. The highway was only four lanes across and had a speed limit of 45 miles per hour; quite the change from highways in Cincinnati where going under 70 mph could get you the finger.

Driving between the two volcanoes of "The Valley Isle", we could see nothing but headlights. On the notoriously beautiful shoreline highway leading to West Maui, we saw nothing but rocks on our right and a black sky to our left, keeping a view of the ocean a mystery until morning. We picked up sandwiches on the way to Honokowai and soon arrived at our oceanfront condo. It was 8:30 p.m. Hawaiian Standard Time; 1:30 a.m. where we had departed a long eighteen hours ago. Thirty minutes later, after showering and eating our sandwiches, we went straight to bed. I was a long way from Cincinnati, where I had lived my whole life, but lying in bed listening to the sound of waves crashing along the shore made me feel right at home.

I awoke the next morning after eleven hours of uninterrupted sleep on the pull-out sofa. Opening my crusted eyes and looking outside from the 5th floor was unforgettable. Shades of green from the palm trees leaped from the light blue of the sky. The ocean was breathtaking, with deep navy hues, glassy looking surface, and overwhelming enormity. I'd never realized how one-dimensional some settings appear, for if Cincinnati was the standard, I was now seeing 3D.

My mom was already awake and sitting on the lanai (Hawaiian for patio) reading a book.

Gazing at the setting I was aspiring to call home I greeted her, "Good morning."

"Good morning," my mom replied. "How is Miranda doing?"

"She's doing better than you would think. I can't wait until she wakes up."

From Mainland to Maui

This morning would be Miranda's first time seeing the Pacific Ocean and the gorgeous land named Maui. After sipping some coffee and waiting patiently for my girlfriend to get out of bed, I decided to wake her.

"Good morning my love," I whispered softly in her ear. "You've been asleep for over eleven hours. It's a beautiful morning if you're ready to get up."

Miranda climbed out of bed and walked outside.

"Good morning Miranda," my mom said. "How did you sleep?"

Miranda stood silently in a trance-like state, soaking in the serene Maui morning and appearing like an innocent child amazed at seeing something for the first time; outwardly shy and timid, yet internally ecstatic.

We all could have been perfectly content lazily gazing at the sea, but we had much to do and time was short. Miranda needed to visit the Outback Steakhouse 45 minutes away in Kihei to finalize her transfer. We also needed to buy a car and find a place to live. Having arrived nearly a week later than planned, we were already behind schedule.

"Why don't we go ahead and go to Outback then pick up some classified ads and start looking for cars?" I said eager to start establishing ourselves.

"Why don't we go to the beach?" Miranda responded. "Let's just take today to relax and then we'll start on that tomorrow."

I was still exhausted from the previous week and it didn't take much convincing for me to put off the "important" stuff for a day. But before the beach we needed some food, meaning it was time for Miranda and

I to come face to face with what we had been told was insanely expensive. We entered the nearest grocery store and began browsing the aisles, noticing that while prices were certainly higher than back in Ohio, many items on sale were priced similar to what we were accustomed. So, we started loading up the cart with only sale items, avoiding the $7 boxes of cereal, $6 microwavable meals, and $2 cups of yogurt.

With our cooler packed, we needed a couple things I viewed as essentials; body boards and snorkel sets. The place to live, car, and jobs would come second to beach gear. I would later discover how this sort of thing gets a lot of people in trouble when trying to relocate to Hawaii. Many people, instead of finding housing, buying transportation and looking for a job, stay in their vacation rental, buy beer, and rent surfboards. In other words, instead of hitting the streets with their resumes, they hit the beach with coolers. So here we were, heading to the beach with a cooler and stopping for body boards on the way. It's not easy arriving at such a notorious vacation destination and choosing work over play.

Finally reaching the sandy parking lot, we couldn't wait to swim in the blue waters and sunbathe on the pristine sand. Unfortunately, our first day at the beach was a horribly miserable time. What started as a clear, calm morning had turned into a cloudy, windy afternoon. The sun had disappeared behind the clouds, the ocean was choppy and the water murky. My mom tried sitting on the beach without being pelted by blowing sand while Miranda and I forced our way into the cold rough water.

Through her trips to the Atlantic Ocean, Miranda had developed a fear of underwater creatures. Without being able to see what may be swimming nearby, she feared sharks, jellyfish, and anything else that could harm her. Before we moved, I had described Hawaii's crystal clear waters as unlike anything she'd ever seen; certainly unlike the Atlantic. I hadn't taken into account that even in Hawaii the weather still changes, and the afternoons can be windy and cloudy, and the ocean muddied with sand.

"This is miserable!" Miranda was livid. "I'm getting out. I'm freezing and I can't see anything under the water!"

"Miranda, it's OK," I said. "Nothing is going to hurt you. Just swim around a little bit and you'll warm up."

As Miranda started making her way back to the beach, I felt horrible. She looked furious and wouldn't talk to me. Not quite the first impression you want to have after moving away to a place you've never been.

In our first days on Maui, we tried to have fun. This was a challenge. Our first time at the beach was anything but entertaining. The first time we went snorkeling Miranda was forced by a wave into some coral and was cut, leaving a permanent scar on her leg. The first time we took a walk it was unbearably hot. Of course back in Ohio I had described the trade winds cooling the afternoon sun, but on the day of our first walk it was 95 degrees with no breeze and intense humidity. Sweating profusely while walking down the street, I pretended not to mind; Maui was my bright idea! With the terrible first impression, Miranda didn't like the island and believed I had fabricated or misinterpreted the realities. She wasn't even sure if she wanted to stay.

All the cars we looked at buying were sold by private owners, and given our $2,000 budget, were in bad shape. After test driving a few which felt as though they could break down at any minute, we found a 12-year-old Ford Taurus. Without knowing anything about cars, it appeared to be in decent shape, so we bought it for $1,350.

David J. Gross

In celebration of buying our new (very used) car, we wanted to see the top of Haleakala; the summit of the dormant volcano emerging over 10,000 feet above sea level. After chugging 7,000 feet up "The House of the Sun", I began to smell something burning. I pulled the car to the side of the road (not being able to check the temperature gauge as it was broken when we bought it) and shut it off. I didn't know much about cars, but knew that steam, smoke, and a strange odor pouring from underneath the hood meant trouble.

Shortly after our car overheated, a tourist couple stopped and offered to take us to the summit and drop us off on their way back. While it was a nice offer, we had planned on staying for a few hours to take a hike. So we gratefully declined their offer, deciding to try and creep our way to the top. After a few minutes of letting the car cool down, the old Ford started up and we slowly made it to the summit.

Getting out of the car, we inhaled the thin crisp air and watched the clouds travel beneath us. We had entered a different world after the two- and half-hour journey. It was like we had stepped foot on the Moon, Mars, or perhaps some ancient land devastated by meteorites. It was cold, desolate, and untouched aside from the observation deck and parking lot lined with shiny clean rental cars. Miranda and I had never been to this high of an elevation, and the views from over 10,000 feet were incredible. With the Big Island of Hawaii in the far distance and the entire island of Maui visible below, we were ecstatic to start hiking. So, with a lunch packed, a gallon of frozen water, and ignorance about the wilderness, we got started.

Strolling into the visitor center, we spoke with the ranger, "Aloha! We're interested in hiking for around three hours. What do you recommend?"

He pointed down to a map, "Well, this is one of the more popular routes. It's about five miles roundtrip and leads down into the crater. That will take about three hours. Just make sure you bring food and plenty of water."

"Oh yeah," I quickly responded, "We're prepared. Thanks for the help."

We opted for leaving our food in the car, planning to have lunch when we returned. I used my old high school book bag to carry our jug of ice and assumed we would have plenty of water as it melted. So down we went: down the trail called "Sliding Sands" into the crater. We swiftly glided down the sandy hill letting gravity do most of the work for us and quickly arrived where the guide had told us to stop and come back. We had made great time making it down in less than an hour.

"Ha!" I laughed. "Great job Miranda! We must have been going twice as fast as everyone else. There's no way this will take us three hours."

We tried drinking some water after taking in the sights of the caldera, but the ice hadn't melted like I expected due to the colder temperatures from the altitude. We finished the last drop of available water and started our trek back up the trail we had so effortlessly descended. By this point the sun had intensified, and we were getting thirstier by the minute. Every step up seemed to slide us back lower than we started, and I now understood why this potentially deadly trail was named "Sliding Sands". What was fun going down became dangerous climbing up, especially being out of shape, unaccustomed to the high elevation, and without water. On our left was a steep hill heading up and out of the crater, while on our right was the opposite where falling could be fatal.

This again was not a good first impression for Miranda having never hiked before in her life. Despite our struggles, we managed to safely make it back and quickly devoured our picnic lunch in the car before falling asleep. We slept long enough for my left knee, the one exposed to the sun shining through the window, to get seriously burnt. I can only imagine what the tourists must have thought seeing us there asleep, already standing out by having the oldest car in the parking lot.

We'd bought a car and were ready to move on to finding a place to call home. But before starting our quest, we decided to once again try snorkeling. The first time Miranda was cut by coral and left with a scar. This time she was left with ear infections in both of her ears. After going to Urgent Care, she received some medicine that wouldn't cure the painful infections for nearly two weeks.

Our first impression of Maui was anything but paradise. Miranda detested the constant heat, was scarred by the ocean, traumatized by our first hike, and now suffered from throbbing pain in both of her ears. Our car broke down trying to reach the summit, and I felt responsible for everything.

Back on the house hunt, we wanted an inexpensive one bedroom condo or ohana, preferably furnished. The first place we visited fit our criteria, but just barely. It was a dark condo that smelled bad with furnishings that should have been replaced years ago. Just looking at the old mattress made my back hurt, and seeing a two inch cockroach lying belly up on our way out verified that this was not where we wanted to call home.

We continued our search which led us to an older Japanese man renting out his attached ohana. For $1000 a month we could park in the driveway, open and walk through his garage, through the back yard, and then finally reach the attached ohana. It was one room, furnished with a full-size bed, table for two, a desk, a tiny bathroom, mini-refrigerator, and microwave. I've stayed at budget hotels that were twice the size. We continued our search.

We then visited a detached ohana in a newer sub-division of Kihei. This one smelled of new carpet, had the tags still attached to the appliances and was immaculately clean. The downsides were that it was more expensive and unfurnished. After some debate, we decided we wanted a furnished rental. While planning our move, we were convinced that we only wanted to live on Maui for one year before returning to the Mainland and didn't want the hassle of buying a bed, couch, and other household items to sell a year later.

The next day we saw an ad in the paper for a one bedroom furnished ohana in Kihei for $1100 per month. The rent included water, trash, electricity, and satellite TV; so, one payment of $1100 each month would cover our place to live. Upon seeing the unit, the place wasn't big, but it was doable. While it wasn't living in luxury, it was just a mile away from Miranda's job, the price was good, and it would enable the lifestyle we had desired on Maui. We hadn't come to Maui to sit inside watching television or decorating our bathroom and kitchen. We wanted to explore the island, have new experiences, be adventurous and create memories. Agreeing that our priorities had nothing to do with where we slept and cooked our meals, we happily signed a six-month lease.

Two weeks quickly vanished, and the time had come for us to take my mom back to the airport. I couldn't thank her enough for the sacrifice, although spending time on Maui isn't too torturous. We said our goodbyes and she disappeared into the crowd of people who were sadly flying home.

My mom's leaving the island gave Miranda and me a strange feeling. We were thousands of miles from everything we were accustomed to, and while it felt liberating, especially at 20 years old, it was kind of weird. Being so far from everything and everyone we'd ever known let us focus on ourselves and who we were, rather than how we'd been perceived. We were able to set aside how others may have affected us and concentrate solely on how we affected ourselves. We could focus on our relationship as a couple while also meditating on who we were as individuals.

Miranda nervously started her new job the next day by first introducing herself to the managers. She was anxious to start, and while she had already worked for Outback, the menu, floor layout, operations, employees, and bosses would all differ. Another thing we would both come to find while working on Maui was the diverse clientele. When waiting tables in Cincinnati the customers were fairly similar; talked with the same accent, had similar income levels, similar preferences, and showed little variety. Here on Maui was the complete opposite. You could be waiting on a laid-back local group, a foreign couple struggling to speak English, and a family visiting from the Mainland all at the same time. We were working in a worldwide tourist destination with all sorts of people from all over the globe.

While Miranda was getting started at Outback, I began applying at different restaurants. In reading about Hawaii's job market, I had anticipated difficulty in being hired as a server. This was another key difference between Cincinnati, Ohio and Maui. To be a restaurant server in Cincinnati was considered mediocre and lowly, making it a relatively easy job to obtain. It didn't pay the best, was physically tiring, required a good amount of patience, and you always smelled like food. But in Hawaii the position of a food server was much different. You still smelled like food, it still required labor and patience, but the pay and customers were much better. Eating out and being on vacation go hand in hand, as does drinking more alcohol than you would at home, and tourists on vacation sipping Mai Tais were friendlier and more generous than over-worked suburban families at home who were simply eating out to avoid cooking.

From Mainland to Maui

Another reason this seemingly below average job was desired in Hawaii was the hours. In Maui, once the sun goes down, you're either drinking at a bar, eating at a restaurant, or at home with your family. However, during the day there's a multitude of activities readily available at any time. Thanks to the consistently beautiful weather, working evenings allowed for surfing, sunbathing, golfing, playing sports, swimming, snorkeling, body boarding, scuba diving, fishing, or anything else you could think of doing when the sun was out.

After a week of job searching, I was having no luck. I was later told how it's difficult getting any job when you first move to Maui. Employers are leery about newcomers remaining on the island, and it's too time-consuming and expensive to train someone who could easily leave in a month.

I initially sought after more upscale restaurants, as was my preference, but eventually considered returning to Outback. I was on Maui to play rather than work, and while this wasn't my first choice, it would pay the bills. It would also be convenient with owning only one car, so the next day I applied at Outback and was hired on the spot.

Miranda and I worked with people from all over the world. Our proprietor was initially from Florida who had recently transferred to Maui from the Bahamas. Some of the cooks and servers were Polynesians who had lived on Maui their entire lives. We worked with people from all over the Mainland, including someone from Dayton, Ohio located just an hour north of Cincinnati. Someone from Colorado was preparing to move to Thailand, while another server was getting ready to move back to her birthplace in Switzerland. A woman from Australia had lived on Maui for three years, and another server had just moved from California. There were even a handful of men from Ireland on a summer work visa.

David J. Gross

It was interesting observing the differences between employees based on how long they'd lived on Maui. I remember talking to a girl from Michigan who had lived on the island for several years who told us that every couple she'd ever seen move to Maui had separated. She said that most couples come to Maui looking for a change, and after a few months of island living, end up discovering they really wanted a different relationship instead of location. Miranda and I didn't take her "warning" too seriously, and even joked about proving her wrong. However, I did understand how such a drastic change could either deepen a relationship or cause extreme conflict.

After a few weeks, Miranda and I really started enjoying the island and all it had to offer. We would work the same five nights every week, going in around five and leaving getting home before ten. We returned to the envelope budgeting system we used in Ohio, only instead of saving money to move to Maui, we were now saving to move back. On our days off we'd have as much fun as time would allow. We'd spend one day at the beach and one day taking an adventure to a different part of the island. One evening we'd go out to eat (usually at Outback, still getting a 50% off employee discount), and the next night we'd borrow a free movie from our landlord's video rental store.

One of the biggest changes in our daily lives while living on Maui was our bedtime. Back in Cincinnati, we didn't feel like there was much to do; at least not outside. Usually the days were dictated by bad weather which made movie watching late at night good entertainment. But in Maui everyday was sunny and warm, and we wanted to hit the beach! We would get home from work, eat a small meal, and then go to bed. We'd go to the beach every morning, and then around two o'clock, we'd go home, shower, eat, and then go to work. That was our routine every "weekday". We were always at the beach; but why not? We could sunbathe, snorkel, play in the waves, talk on the phone, read books, listen to music, and do almost anything you could do elsewhere.

From Mainland to Maui

The beach was our second home, and if we weren't sleeping or working, that's where we were.

We were living in a dream; the dream I had dreamt while in Cincinnati bundling up to drive to work when it was 15 degrees Fahrenheit. We now gazed at the majestic volcanoes I had envisioned every time I made spaghetti for dinner in our old apartment. We listened to the waves I had longed to hear while back on the mainland, getting ready for bed and hearing the television from the apartment beneath us. On sticky smoldering days in Ohio, when it was too hot and humid to go outside, I longed for the breezy trade winds we now felt daily. We hadn't been on Maui for more than a month and it already felt like home. Everyday we'd smell the air, feel the sand beneath our feet, see the beauty of the land, and listen to the sound of waves collapsing along the shoreline. And every day we felt alive.

David J. Gross

5. A GLIMPSE OF SUCCESS

We lived in a fantasyland during our first three months on Maui. One day Miranda and I went snorkeling and encountered several Hawaiian green sea turtles gliding through the water. In the midst of admiring their gracefulness and beauty, two manta rays then appeared in the distance. The visibility of the water was crystalline, showcasing the mammoth wingspans of these underwater giants. Miranda and I knew what they were, but we didn't know whether to relax and enjoy the experience, or fear for our lives. We weren't aware that despite their size, appearing as if they could swallow us whole, manta rays simply open their mouths to swallow plankton for food. Our nerves settled once they turned and began swimming into the deeper blue of the ocean. Looking to my left were rays, to my right were turtles.

What a place to call home!

We aspired for one "adventure" every week, either visiting another part of the island or trying something new. Whether it was hiking, taking a paid tour, or just driving to explore, we were determined to experience Maui and all it had to offer. We challenged ourselves to do things we wouldn't have done, or didn't have a chance to do, while living in Cincinnati. We had the same feeling that people have while on vacation; a childlike curiosity with fewer reservations than one might have at home, and a greater willingness to try new things.

One of the first hikes we read about easily matched our idea of adventure. It described a trail that crept through a bamboo forest to a waterfall, climbing a steep muddy hill to another waterfall, climbing an old rope to then boulder hop until ending at a pool. After swimming a few hundred yards and climbing a smaller waterfall, the trail ended with a magnificent forty-foot waterfall as final reward.

Soon after starting the hike, Miranda and I quickly became lost and spent the next thirty minutes muscling through dense bamboo while avoiding spider webs as best we could. Back on the trail, we hopped a couple of streams and then arrived at the first waterfall. Climbing the hill to the left and making it to the second wasn't too hard but climbing to the third was a different story.

Miranda had always been afraid of heights, and this was not a casual walk up the side of a hill. This was a sheer rock slope with a few shallow indentions, forcing complete reliance on an old rope.

"Dave, I don't think I can do this," Miranda said in fear.

"Let's just give it a try, and if you can't make it to the top we'll go back. I'll help you up as far as I can, and I'll be right here."

I hoisted Miranda halfway up as she clung to the lifeline of unknown origin.

"If I get to the top, will you be able to make it up?" Miranda asked with her entire body shaking as she looked down.

Convincing her I would follow, she safely made it to the top of the cliff. I reluctantly kept my word by doing the same, and then after boulder hopping and swimming, we reached our destination. Being alone at the fourth and final waterfall, we stripped off our clothes and jumped into the frigid pool of water in celebration. The setting was beautiful and serene, with lush greenery encompassing the cathedral-like rock formations. The waterfall finale was spectacular, but it was braving the rope and getting lost at the start that made the adventure.

Life on Maui was paradise. Not only were we having an extraordinary time with all sorts of activities, we were also saving money. The majority of what we did was free, and what did cost money was relatively inexpensive through being a Hawaii resident. Kama'aina (local) discounts were another perk to living in Hawaii, and another thing providing affordability. We would simply show our Hawaii ID's for whale watches, snorkel trips, and even zip-lining for a good percentage off the regular price. Shopping at Costco saved us money too; although eating the same meals did get old.

And we only bought food and essentials. In the eight months we lived on Maui we never bought a single article of clothing, electronic, or toy. We didn't need them. Our entertainment was the beach, and while most people we knew were spending money at bars, we were in bed so we could wake up early to enjoy the next day. We were making twice the money we did in Ohio and spending less than expected, and when checking our budget found we were actually saving more money than ever before! We were working 25 hours a week, living on Maui, making wonderful memories, and saving money.

Back in Cincinnati, Miranda's oldest brother was handling their mother's estate. Miranda and I were aware that Miranda would be receiving some inheritance money, but had no idea of the amount. One day Miranda unexpectedly received a check in the mail for several tens of thousands of dollars from a life insurance policy. We didn't need the money and Miranda didn't want a car, vacation, new clothes or jewelry, and viewed the money as security for the future. So, without touching a dime, she decided to deposit the largest check either one of us had ever seen into a one-year certificate of deposit at the bank.

From Mainland to Maui

Getting a big check in the mail would give most people an ear-to-ear grin, yet it gave Miranda mixed emotions. She didn't know what to think or how to feel. She somewhat felt like a sell-out; like someone was trying to make a deal. Like someone was saying, "I know it's hard that your mom died, but here's some money to make it alright." She knew the thought was silly, but still felt cheated. She didn't want the money, she wanted her mom. She would have shredded the check and gleefully tossed its remnants in the air for just one last phone call.

You would think that two twenty-year-olds would buy at least something, but nothing changed after receiving the money. I remember driving our '95 Ford Taurus with its broken temperature gauge and seeing a brand-new yellow Corvette.

"That's a nice car," Miranda said. "I could buy that today if I wanted to."

It was surreal at the age of twenty to have enough money to travel the world, put a down payment on a house, or purchase an exotic sports car. To spend a thousand dollars on a shopping spree wouldn't have made a significant dent, but we didn't. We could have planned a vacation, but we didn't. In viewing all the things money could buy we didn't want any of them. We had struggled, worked hard, saved money and lived simply for an entire year to be rewarded with a permanent vacation; only interrupted by working five hours a day, five days a week. All the money in the world couldn't have bought the amount of pride, satisfaction, and appreciation we had earned through our efforts, and every dollar Miranda inherited would remain untouched.

Three months of living in paradise had passed when things began to feel different. We started waking up with less urgency to hit the beach and began running out of new things to see and do. We were accustomed to the constant opportunity to view the ocean and were getting tired of the same meals from Costco. Maui began feeling more like reality and less like the dream world we had fallen in love with. I had felt a sort of high from the move, the new town, the new people, and new job; but now I was coming down. My adventuresome spirit was weakening, encouraging me to think of returning to the Mainland.

I had always been interested in business and entrepreneurship throughout my life. Even at the age of 14, I used my mom's credit card to set up an Ebay account where I'd buy and sell for a profit, so, when thinking about returning to the Mainland, I started reading books on investing, real estate, the stock market, and business management. I began preparing myself to return to "the real world". While I never desired much of what money could buy, I wanted money as a way to show success. I had always viewed money like points, and the more points I earned the better player I was in the game of business; and in the game of life. From what I'd inadvertently learned while growing up, the more money you have, the more successful you are. I wanted to be successful, so I wanted to make a lot of money.

One night at work I asked a few of the older Outback employees, "What do you think is the key to success?"

A man with back pain from waiting tables his whole life said, "Never cheat on your back, and never cheat on your feet!"

I asked one of the bartenders, "What would you say is the key to success?"

"Keep it simple," he said. "When I was younger, I lived in Florida and spent a lot of time trying to figure everything out. But now, for me anyway, I just try to keep it simple. It works for me, but if someone wanted to be rich that probably wouldn't work too well."

I listened to his idea of keeping it simple, but to me this "key to success" lacked ambition and was downright lazy. Why keep it simple when you can work hard, get rich, make a name for yourself and get ahead?

That was my mindset when I was twenty. I was young, smart and ambitious, ready to seize the world. That was at twenty. I'd later view what I perceived as an unmotivated mentality of accepting mediocrity as some of the best advice I'd ever receive.

It was nearing August when we received a call from Miranda's dad informing us that he was getting remarried. The wedding would be on New Year's Eve in Louisville, Kentucky, about two hours south of Cincinnati. With Miranda committed to attending the wedding, we were faced with a choice: we could leave Maui, be in Cincinnati for the holidays before attending the wedding and then move somewhere closer to family, or; visit with family for a couple weeks, attend the wedding, and then return to Maui. However, with the holiday season being the busiest time on Maui for tourism, time off work was an issue. We worked for a corporation with strict policies regarding the holidays, and if we left, we'd most likely return unemployed.

After weighing our options, we decided to move back to the Mainland, saving us money and the hassle with work. Uneasy about cutting our time short on Maui, yet submitting to our decision, we put the issue to rest. We would fly back "home" in less than four months.

We continued making as many memories as possible before leaving, and while most of our adventures were flawlessly spectacular, some were not. There's a Redwood forest on Maui only accessible by one, four-mile long road, beginning with a sign- "4-Wheel Drive ONLY". We owned a low-riding 4-door sedan, but stubbornly went anyway. After roughing three miles over protruding rocks and gaping holes we heard a loud scrape causing the car to stall a minute later. Not only did I know nothing about cars, but it was raining, and we were completely alone in the forest.

After waiting a couple of minutes, the car surprisingly started. We managed to make it a few hundred yards closer to the park before it again shut off. Assuming it would need towed, we decided to delay the inevitable and enjoy our day in the forest. We spent the next two hours hiking before returning to our overworked and broken-down car. Putting the key in the ignition, we had no reason to believe it would start, but it did! Deloras (our nickname for our first joint car) had recovered, and despite the clutch slipping the whole drive back, we carefully made it home.

Upon returning to Kihei, we noticed a red liquid dripping from the car. It was Sunday, and with every auto repair shop closed, we parked on the street next to the repair shop hoping to be looked at in the morning. I was angry, not because of our car, but because we had failed to use common sense. I suppose when expectations are high it's easy to ignore the facts while hoping the reality will somehow change. We knew we shouldn't have taken that road, and the mistake would cost us.

After miserably walking home, we noticed our landlords putting a new roof on the house. Pounding hammers could be heard from the end of our street, and approaching the door of our ohana, we could only imagine the noise inside. All we wanted to do was to go inside and rest from our exhausting and stressful day, but instead we came home to the noise of pounding hammers. The next few days would not be fun.

After getting a ride to work the following afternoon we noticed Miranda wasn't assigned to any tables in the restaurant. We both assumed someone had misread the schedule when making the table chart, so Miranda went back to the manager's office to let them know. This is when our carefree routine was seemingly destroyed.

First, to give a little background: A few weeks earlier our store's proprietor had fallen down some stairs and was bedridden, requiring a manager from Oahu to come fill in. The man taking our proprietor's place was in his twenties and decided to bring his waitress girlfriend along, treating the time on Maui as a vacation. Miranda hadn't gotten along with this couple as they openly abused their situation of working together.

While Miranda was heading back to the office, I was already waiting on a table and gearing up for a busy night. Minutes later, Miranda came out of the office in tears. She had been fired without reason and was told to leave the premises, so she went outside and cried. I followed her and tried to console her by assuring that everything would be fine, but I was irate! I wanted to walk back in the restaurant and deck the little punk with everything in me, spitting on the ground as I left; but I didn't. I figured that's probably what he wanted me to do. So Miranda got a ride home while I worked the rest of the night barely speaking a word. After dozens of forced smiles to hungry families, I sprinted home. I was never a runner, but for those two miles you would have thought I ran track.

I suppose the saying's true, at least in our situation, that "when it rains it pours". We woke up to banging on our roof the next morning, limited to going to wherever was in walking distance. Miranda had been unjustifiably fired, and we were leaving Maui in a short couple of months.

A few noisy, immobile, and unemployed days later, everything was resolved. The roofing completed, our car was repaired, and Miranda was guaranteed her job back when the proprietor returned. So, after sorting things over the phone with the permanent boss, Miranda enjoyed her time off and returned to work two weeks later. We were told soon after that the fill-in manager who had fired Miranda was no longer employed by Outback and was moving back to the Mainland single.

It was September, our birthdays were just over a month away, and our money envelopes were full. We had saved much more than we spent, leaving more than enough cash to get re-established on the Mainland. With a desire to see every major Hawaiian Island before moving, we decided to take a birthday cruise. Departing a week after our 21st birthdays (mine being 11 days after Miranda's), we would board the *Pride of Aloha* from Maui and spend seven nights cruising the Hawaiian Islands. It would be a convenient way to see the islands, a nice way to treat ourselves for our hard work of saving money.

On the first day she could legally drink alcohol, Miranda wanted to take a snorkeling trip that advertised frequent dolphin sightings off the island of Lana'i. We woke up early with much to look forward to, only to find it storming. It rarely rains in Kihei, but today was unfortunately one of the few yearly occasions. Any other day we would have loved the rain, but not today. Believing our boat trip would certainly be cancelled, we went to the harbor anyway. The trip wasn't cancelled, but the itinerary was altered, visiting a snorkel spot we'd repeatedly been to, so we took the option to reschedule and spent the day inside watching movies. We took the trip a couple days later and, despite not seeing dolphins, had a fabulous time.

Standing on the 4th hole of a golf course gazing up at the West Maui Mountains was where I enjoyed my first beer (legally). After a round of golf, we continued my birthday celebration by checking in to the historic Pioneer Inn in Lahaina. We then walked across the street for a sunset cocktail cruise. On the boat, we instinctively went to the bow to comfortably sprawl on the catamaran's trampoline. Lying on the front of the boat while drinking cold beers and listening to an acoustic guitarist playing soothing Hawaiian music was the greatest birthday I could have imagined.

We met another passenger from Cincinnati on board and told him we were residents, leading him to ask, "So what, is this like your idea of dinner and movie when living on Maui? An evening cruise having drinks for your Friday night out?"

"Well," I replied, "It beats watching a movie, and honestly, it's about the same price. But no, today is my birthday."

"Happy birthday," he responded, puzzled and intrigued that a young couple from Cincinnati was living on Maui.

Dinner and a movie couldn't compare to being rocked by the waves and serenaded by music on a boat. Just when I thought life could not possibly improve we spotted two bottlenose dolphins swimming directly toward us. Miranda and I watched in silent appreciation while a mother and her calf swam under the bow, giving a spectacular display before swimming away.

By the time we returned to the harbor, we were both tipsy. Miranda had been drinking Mai Tais while I stuck with beer, taking advantage of the boat's open bar. Once leaving the harbor, we had drinks at a couple of bars before eating dinner, and a few hours later were ready for bed.

The next morning, we drove to the north side of West Maui to a part of the island we rarely visited. After grabbing some sandwiches, we started looking for a place to picnic, but we never found a park, picnic table, or even a bench. Instead, I pulled our car to the side of the road overlooking a picturesque bay. Climbing over the guard rail, I set up our beach chairs (kept in the trunk at all times) on the ledge to enjoy our lunch. We could see for miles on the horizon, and looking down we saw coral and sea turtles, even from atop a one-hundred-foot cliff! I never would have imagined a lunchmeat sandwich could taste so good. It was one of the best meals I've ever eaten; deli meat on wheat. I've eaten at several very nice restaurants, but our ocean view picnic was more memorable than any of them.

While our birthdays were officially over, our gift to each other was just ahead. We had wanted to take a cruise for over a year and were ecstatic with finally being of age. I most likely was more excited than Miranda, for I had planned for more than just a cruise. Over the course of three years I had fallen deeply in love with my girlfriend, feeling as though I never wanted to be without her. I had secretly purchased an engagement ring a few months earlier and had been waiting for the perfect moment to propose. I had tried before; on an early morning at the summit of Haleakala to watch the sunrise, but after the two- and half-hour drive to the top (luckily with no car trouble this time) we found ourselves in the middle of a rain cloud and couldn't see a thing. So, proposing would have to wait until the cruise.

We parked at the airport and took a cab to the pier. Despite being smaller and older in comparison to many cruise ships, we viewed the vessel as extraordinary. Some people complained about the slightly worn and dated ship, but we were thrilled. We were twenty-one years old on a cruise ship set to explore the Hawaiian Islands; and I was proposing in three days.

Boarding the ship and standing outside on the 11th deck I gazed in awe at Maui's mountains, clear blue skies, and expansive ocean. This was my reality. This was the life, and I was living. For a moment I thought of my revelation in college standing outside smoking a cigarette in the cold. It was the beginning of November with the weather as good as could be. I didn't even want to know what the weather was presently like in Cincinnati. Then I thought about the change December would bring by returning to the Mainland.

Trying not to start our vacation by anxiously thinking about our future move, I observed the other passengers. In looking at the group, it was obvious most were enjoying their retirement. I thought about the many years they'd spent working so they could now, old and wrinkled, lay by the pool sipping Pina Coladas. At some point they were healthy and active, but now, in Hawaii, with tons of activities available, many struggled to remain standing and needed to cling onto railings as they walked.

Looking around and talking with Miranda about the retired majority, we both felt we had cheated the system. Comparing ourselves with what most twenty-one-year-olds do for their birthdays, we felt like we had uncovered a secret back door we weren't supposed to walk through until years down the road. Being the youngest and paying attention to the passengers on board, we felt they viewed us the same way. Maybe it was in our head, but they seemed to look us up and down with a concerned look on their face like we had broken a rule. Then, after having conversations revealing where we lived, just twenty minutes south of where the cruise ship was docked, an expression of utter perplexity filled their faces. When telling one of the Mainland tourists we lived on Maui you could tell they had questions but were unclear of what to ask. Sometimes they'd ask if we had moved to Maui for a job or military, but our answers seemed to block any other questions. Maui was the best place I'd ever been, and Miranda trusted my taste. That's why we moved and that's what we answered.

We were young, healthy, and thrilled to see new places, including our first stop of Oahu; home of famous Waikiki Beach. Exiting the ship, our first stop was to the bar to watch our beloved Cincinnati Bengals take on the San Diego Chargers. After a typical Cincinnati loss, we ate lunch and walked to Waikiki Beach. This was our first time seeing the world-renowned landmark; and we were far from impressed. We've since come to appreciate the area as a more beautiful version of South Beach, Florida, but detested the hurried "Mainland" feel at the time. Knowing we'd get plenty of that the next month, we returned to the ship and spent the rest of the day lying by the pool.

We woke up the next morning to a beautifully clear morning off the coast of Kauai, with scattered clouds slowly drifting above the lush mountains. It would be a perfect day for our helicopter tour, and we couldn't wait to see the island from the sky; and I couldn't wait to propose.

A shuttle picked us up from the pier and took us to the airport for what was to be our first helicopter ride. For the next hour we witnessed indescribable beauty I cannot begin to portray in words, bringing Miranda and I both to tears. What I felt while circling the smallest of Hawaii's main islands with its countless waterfalls, exquisite colors, breathtaking mountains, and serene sandy beaches was a spiritual experience I'll never forget.

Back on the ground we rented a convertible. I drove north while Miranda fell asleep from the lazily winding road and gentle breeze. Once Miranda woke from her nap, I parked near Hanalei Bay, deeming it the ideal spot to propose. Waterfalls cascaded the mountains in the distance as we walked the long crescent shaped coastline of fine white sand before sitting down on our beach towels. After a few minutes of taking in the new sights, I reached down and pulled out a wooden box containing a solitaire diamond engagement ring.

I had never been so nervous showing Miranda the symbol when asking, "Miranda, will you marry me?"

"Yes!" she gleefully said, bringing us both to tears.

From Mainland to Maui

After gaining ten pounds, seeing lava glowing at night on the Big Island, finding "our song" while dancing on the night of our engagement and then getting lots of free champagne for the occasion, we sailed back to Maui. Back home, we put in our notice to leave work and planned to spend a week on Kauai before returning to the Mainland.

We spent the week of Thanksgiving away from our family (a first for us both), in a cottage on Kauai near our engagement spot. Spending time on Kauai was something we had both wanted to do before leaving the state, and now was our final chance. Time stood still that week. Each morning we were awakened by the crowing of roosters and then fell asleep at night to wind rustling the palms outside. While there obviously wasn't a more special event than our engagement, we had a magnificent week. We spent our days hiking, lying on various beaches and driving around spotting waterfalls. At night, we'd soak in a hot tub before going to bed. We loved Kauai and found the island hard to leave, but ending a vacation flying back to Maui wasn't too bad!

With only a couple weeks left in Hawaii I began persuading myself that leaving was for the best. But deep down I loved living on Maui and didn't want to leave, so I began resenting everyone on the island. I told myself that the people on Maui were all adults who didn't want to grow up. The people in their 40's who drove rusty cars, waited tables for a living, drank beer on their days off, and viewed surfing as all-important were wrong. These people never talked about getting ahead in life. They wouldn't discuss retirement, the stock market, business and finance. They wanted to "talk story", soak up the sun and play in the waves. Most of the people I knew didn't own a house and had no problem paying rent. Some didn't even have a savings account, and many didn't mind living paycheck to paycheck. I convinced myself that living on Maui was irresponsible, and I viewed myself as better.

David J. Gross

I mentally justified leaving for many reasons: We couldn't afford to buy a house, it was too far away from family, there weren't many "real jobs", we couldn't raise a child with the expenses, etc. Everything I had been told convinced me that life on the Mainland was the best option and perhaps the only realistic one. It's true, houses are expensive on Maui, and it was far away from family, yet the allure remained strong in my heart. I knew I wanted to stay, regardless of how impractical it seemingly appeared.

We had big plans and wanted a house, careers, and children in the future. While we had explored Hawaii making wonderful and lasting memories (while saving money working just 25 hours a week), we were ready to get back to reality. I remember repeatedly telling myself that life on Maui was not "the real world". We were engaged to be married and eager to start our life together. We planned to go back to Cincinnati for the holidays, attend the wedding in Kentucky, then find a city close to home where we could "settle down". We would leave to pursue the coveted "American Dream".

I had ambition, financial goals, and plans for moving up in the world. Miranda wanted to be a stay-at-home mom, cooking and taking care of the kids. So, for the last two weeks we lived on Maui our future plans were all we could think about. You would think being without a job for the last two weeks of our eight-month stay would be great, but it wasn't. While you would think we'd have made the best of our final days on Maui, we didn't, and instead spent most of our time inside watching TV. We ignored our deep sadness about leaving the island and never discussed our deepest emotion. We just continued trying to convince ourselves how great things would be once we were established on the Mainland.

A few days before leaving we sold our car for $1300; only $50 less than we had paid. When the older woman buying the car handed us the cash, she also gave us a box of macadamia nut chocolates and a card wishing us luck in moving. We rented a car for the last couple days in Kihei, finished our packing, and gave away some of our things to a friend.

Our last evening in paradise was beautiful, with every element in place for a stunning sunset. After stuffing our rental car with our luggage, we went to the beach for the last few moments of sunlight. While already showered and dressed for the flight, I saw everyone enjoying the beach; swimming, reading, and sunbathing. Every person wearing board shorts or a bikini seemed to mock the fact that we were leaving. I wanted to strip off my pants and collared shirt and run wildly into the ocean, shredding my plane ticket as it flew in the breeze. I wanted to cry. I wanted to scream. But in that moment, all I could really ask was to be able to enjoy our final evening. I wanted to relish our last Maui sunset, but I couldn't.

After a couple minutes of sitting and mentally recapping the last eight months I started tearing up. Miranda already had tears running down her face as she tried not to ruin her make-up. With watery eyes and blurred vision, I hated the sunset. I didn't want to think about what we were leaving any longer. I didn't want to see the many people on the beach who were getting to stay, and I didn't want to see the ocean I had fallen in love with. Miranda was in complete agreement as she sniffled, feeling that watching the sunset only made things worse. So, wiping our eyes, we left the beach.

We must have looked like the saddest people on Maui walking into the restaurant we had chosen for our last meal before flying, and even had to explain to our waitress why we looked so miserable. Our food tasted terrible, and while driving to the airport we were silent. We had nothing good to say, so we said nothing. There was nothing to say. Our instincts told us to cancel the trip and spend the night lying on the beach stargazing, but we didn't. Instead, we lied to ourselves, saying that to permanently reside in the world we'd fallen in love with was not doable; not for such a responsible couple.

Walking into the airport terminal felt like walking down death row after the final meal. On the airplane, we fit in with the other solemn passengers who were primarily tourists ending their vacations. They too were going back to the real world; to their own reality of bills, jobs, problems, and obligations. The plane doors closed, shutting us off from the sweet air I had grown so accustomed to breathing, and when the plane left the runway, Miranda began to bawl. She hadn't cried that hard since hearing the news that her mom had died.

We were getting what we wanted by going back to what we viewed as the "real world". We were doing what we thought best, despite what we felt deep down. We would be doing what we were supposed to do and what we'd been told was ideal; having careers, living close to family, and working hard to gain financial independence.

It would take me over two years to understand how I had been deceived into believing that life couldn't be as good as we had it on Maui. We had achieved success, yet mistakenly defined it as an interruption from reality. We viewed the experience like a break from true life to experience something different; something other than normal day-to-day living.

If only daily life on the Mainland could be as good as it was on Maui. If only the real world could feel so alive.

DING! "Welcome to Baltimore Washington International Airport...Gateway to the real world...The local time is...

6. Buying "The American Dream"

Miranda wrapped herself in a blanket as we walked to the baggage claim of the Baltimore airport. Only eight months had passed since we left, but it felt like years. Hundreds of people scrambled around talking on their cell phones, while others sat immersed in their computers, books, and newspapers. Advertisements were everywhere, screaming for attention through flat screen televisions with bright, flashy images. The intercom resounded through every airport speaker, "Thank you for your attention. The Travel Security Administration has issued a terrorist threat level of orange…"

Flying overnight from Maui to Baltimore felt like we had landed in a world of chaos. As I walked and smelled a woman's perfume, the deep fryer of a restaurant, and the polish from a shoeshine stand, I remembered the floral scent of the Kahului airport. Where the airport on Maui had seemed quiet and relaxed, BWI felt just the opposite.

We collected our luggage and walked outside. As I looked for my mom, brother, and step-dad who were picking us up, I couldn't help noticing the sound of car horns. In Hawaii, car horns are rarely used and viewed as rude, impolite, or impatient. Greeting my family and loading our luggage into their minivan, I noticed the smell of exhaust fumes from the cars lining the passenger pick-up area. We'd be staying with them in Maryland before making our way to Cincinnati and climbing into the back seat we were shivering from the cold. It was a mild 50 degrees Fahrenheit, but to us it felt frigid. Many people wore short sleeved shirts while we were bundled for a blizzard, even keeping our hats and gloves on during a grocery store visit on the way to their house.

We spent the next few days getting Miranda's car back in working condition. When first reunited with her old car that she'd been given for her 16th birthday, the Mitsubishi Eclipse barely started. Having been stored in Maryland for over eight months, the brakes were also rusted and hardly able to slow the car. After a welcome back repair bill and some time with my family, we drove back to Cincinnati.

Christmas came fast, and knowing we would be homeless and traveling back to the Mainland around the holidays, we were prepared with gifts. We had taken some of our best pictures from Maui and made small photo albums for everyone. Through our time on Maui, we no longer viewed toys and clothes as important, and had gained a greater appreciation for relationships, time, and experiences.

The holiday season was bustling with the shopping and decorating done instinctively in mid-December. Miranda and I had always enjoyed the holidays, but this year was different. We both missed her mom terribly, and Cincinnati didn't feel like home without her. Not only was Lori gone, but my mom and younger brother were staying in Maryland while my older brother was staying at his home in Florida.

The next week we rode with Miranda's brothers and sister-in-law to Kentucky where her dad would be remarried on New Year's Eve. While Miranda liked her dad's fiancé, watching the wedding still brought her to tears. She couldn't help picturing how Lori must have looked on the day of her wedding.

The first weeks back on the Mainland were not fun. The weather was cold and gray, and we couldn't wait to leave. With the holiday season over, it was time for us to begin our search for the perfect place to settle down. We wanted to live somewhere with parks, a good climate, and a good economy. We wanted a place with good schools for our future children, a low crime rate, and a low cost of living. Back in Hawaii I had researched the best places to live through books and articles, and one that consistently ranked high was Raleigh, North Carolina.

Raleigh had several decent parks and a rising economy with great job potential. It was also within a day's drive of our family, the Appalachian Mountains, and the Atlantic Ocean. So we packed up the car and began our hunt for a place to call home. We didn't have a clue of where we would end up, but just knew we didn't want to live in Cincinnati. I had mapped a route leading through Tennessee to North Carolina, then south along the East coast. From there we would drive to Florida and head west if we still couldn't find the ideal place.

We drove through Kentucky and Tennessee before stopping in Asheville, North Carolina for the night. Asheville was beautiful, and while the weather was cool and rainy, the encompassing mountains seemed to warm the entire city. After checking into a cheap hotel and unloading our luggage, we hopped back in the car to explore this city nestled in the hills. We drove through the quaint and seemingly historical downtown before eating at a pizza buffet, immediately noticing the friendly attitude of the people. They seemed peaceful, polite, and genuinely happy.

The next morning, we drove to Raleigh, ranked one of the best places in the United States to live. We first drove through a suburb, then visited a large shopping mall trying to get a feel for the people. While we couldn't see anything truly negative, the whole city seemed to lack character. We continued our search for something unique about this popular city by driving downtown. There were nice areas and bad areas of Raleigh, as is the case in most places. It was the downtown of a big city, and nothing about it impressed us. It didn't appear dirty, overly crowded, or crime-ridden, just bland.

We spent the entire afternoon driving the streets, highways, and alleys in disappointment. Raleigh was a city with a downtown, restaurants, stores, malls, apartments, houses, skyscrapers, people; and a city that could have been any city in the United States. We had read such wonderful things about Raleigh; that the people were nice, the job market booming, and the weather mild. And while all those things may have been true, it had a common trait shared by the vast majority of cities in America. Just like New York, Los Angeles, Cincinnati, St. Louis, or any other big city I've seen pictures of or visited, the city had severed nearly all ties with nature. Nobody was outside, because there was no outside. There weren't people jogging and riding bikes, but rather people driving with the car windows rolled up. The only time people were outside was when they were walking to or from a parking lot. Highways, subdivisions, and retail stores had replaced the forests and natural beauty that once stood dominant, and it felt unnatural being surrounded by nothing but man-made things. Nature is natural, as even the word professes. That's when I understood how Maui was different.

In our struggle to find our home, we automatically compared Raleigh to Maui. Maui had kept thousands of acres of land untouched. On Maui, the land ruled, and its people were responsible for preserving and nurturing that which gave life. Maui was an island, a small piece of land that people worked for and were blessed by in return; and Raleigh lacked this presence of nature we had grown so accustomed to.

Realizing that natural beauty was something we highly valued, we thought back to Asheville. The mountains were a presence of nature similar to the Pacific Ocean on Maui. The city was also just a six-hour drive to Cincinnati. Encouraged by the mountains, streams, waterfalls, wildlife and close proximity to family, we decided to move to Asheville.

The next day we started apartment shopping in the city where we planned to settle down, find lasting careers, and raise kids. After seeing two apartments, we decided to look at one more before getting a hotel for the night. Upon walking into the leasing office, we saw a man, around thirty years old, staring at his computer screen. Slowly glancing up, he pushed his glasses higher on his nose and sat upright to greet us. Nearing the end of his work day, he didn't even bother standing to shake our hands.

"Hi," the man said as he intuitively began pulling out forms for us to fill out. "Do you have a certain price range?" The man showed no emotion.

"Well, we're not really sure," I said. "We just started looking today."

"Okay," he said as he typed on his computer. "Well did you want a one bedroom, two bedrooms, do you have pets?"

"Probably a one bedroom. We just moved from Maui and we're looking to settle down here in Asheville and..."

"Did you say Maui?" the man looked up from his computer.

"Yes."

"I used to live on Maui!" the man said enthusiastically. "It was when I was in my early twenties! Look at this."

He turned his computer screen displaying a Maui sunset, "I look at this picture all day long wishing I could go back. I moved there with just a backpack and a couple hundred bucks, but life was good. Those pineapples were so sweet, and the surfing was great!"

"You could always move back if you wanted," I said.

"No," he snapped back. "I lived a simple life when I was there, and now I'm engaged. My fiancé would never go for it. I've talked to her about it, but her family's here and she wants us to buy a house once we get married."

The energetic conversation ended abruptly as he transformed back to the mundane leasing agent we initially met. Walking past the numbered buildings and showing us a newly painted one-bedroom unit, he quietly discussed Maui as if we were part of a club.

"Did you ever go to Ho'okipa? I lived right around there; in Haiku. Where'd you live?"

"We lived in Kihei."

"Where'd you work?"

"We were both servers in a restaurant. You?"

"I would just do odd jobs and never really had a permanent place to live. I had my backpack with a tent and slept wherever; under a tree, on the beach, or in a friend's yard."

We didn't rent the apartment, but our time was far from wasted, for it was the first time I noticed the difference between a person being himself and pretending to be someone else. That man had shattered the status quo of the masses and lived bravely enough to have nothing; not even food for his next meal. When I saw his computer monitor and listened to him describing where I had been just one month prior, I could see how adventurous of a person he was. But it was only a glimpse. The majority of the time he wasn't himself and did his job secretly unhappy while wanting a different life. I met two different people that day, and it's a day I'll never forget.

The following morning, after our continental breakfast in another budget hotel, we found our home. It was a one bedroom on the top floor with vaulted ceilings and a gas fireplace. The complex had two community swimming pools, a fitness center, and an adjacent bike trail. Excited to find a place we could feel proud of, we impulsively signed a one-year lease, convinced the town of Asheville would be our home for many years to come.

We celebrated the beginning of our new venture over dinner at what would become one of our favorite restaurants and splurged on a $70 hotel room. The next morning, we drove back to Cincinnati and rented a van to move some things which had belonged to Miranda's mom; some furniture, a TV, and a washer and dryer set which Miranda had kept stored in Cincinnati.

We slept on the ground the first few nights in our apartment. We were back to square one; without a bed, without a couch, without jobs, and only one car. Needless to say, we had some work to do, but we didn't mind. We were excited about all of the new stuff we were getting ready to buy. With our low overhead in Maui, we'd saved a good amount of money to be used on a second car and new furniture. So before finding jobs, our full-time commitment was shopping. We bought cookware, plates, toilet paper, and a shower liner; and then we moved on to the fun stuff.

Once we could cook a meal and clean the toilet, we went to the mattress store and bought a heavenly king size mattress and box spring. Next it was onto the furniture store where we bought a double reclining sofa and loveseat set with three tables. We decided to hold off on any other major purchases until we were ready to buy a house;

something we wanted relatively soon. We didn't want to spend money on something that wouldn't work for our future permanent home. Soon after splurging on a great mattress and living room set, I bought a nice used car. After driving an old 1995 Ford Taurus for eight months, this 2003 Nissan Altima with heated leather seats, upgraded stereo system, and many other luxury features was phenomenal.

When it was time to find a job, we didn't have much trouble. Miranda was hired for a serving job close to home in Arden while I went to a restaurant in Asheville. Jobs weren't a big priority, and we planned to wait tables until we were acquainted with the city before finding something more permanent.

One thing that was a first priority for us both was losing weight. Before moving to Maui, we had envisioned jogging down the beach, swimming in the ocean, and getting plenty of exercise. We had pictured pineapple fields and mango trees and believed a healthy lifestyle would come naturally; but we were wrong. While we did spend a lot of time outside, our time was spent sitting on the beach eating unhealthy food. At the grocery store we valued cost and quantity over health and quality, and junk food is much cheaper than healthy food. So we ate waffles with butter and syrup for breakfast, mayonnaise covered burgers for lunch, and fried chicken salads for dinner. On our weekly restaurant outing we inhaled piles of cheese fries with bacon, served with bowls of ranch dressing; one bowl for each of us.

Determined to lose the weight we had gained the previous year, we utilized the complex's fitness center and walking trail daily. We also took hikes in the mountains, taking advantage of the 500 miles of trails surrounding the city. Hiking was an inexpensive and fun way to explore the mountains and spend time together while getting exercise.

From Mainland to Maui

A few weeks later we were comfortable with our jobs, acquainted with our new city, and were enjoying what now felt like home. One day, during our fitness routine, we began discussing our wedding. Where would it take place? How much would it cost? How long we would need to plan?

The biggest questions included where and when the wedding would take place. We ruled out Asheville, not wanting to inconvenience our families by having them visit a city we barely knew. We discussed getting married near Miranda's family in Iowa, but Miranda had moved away when she was very young, and the only time I had been to Iowa was for her mom's funeral. An obvious option was Cincinnati, but weather greatly affected us, and unless it was one of the few days of the year with blue skies and moderate temperatures, it would most likely be either too cold or too hot. After reviewing our options, we realized the island we had fallen in love with was the only fitting place for our marriage to begin. We would get married on Maui.

Miranda had always dreamt of a big wedding with 300 pairs of eyes watching her walk down the aisle. Having a large family, she was accustomed to big weddings and wanted an elaborate wedding dress and reception with tons of food, gifts, and dancing. But, after our time on Maui, she viewed these things as trivial, feeling the price you spend on a wedding doesn't affect the outcome or prosperity of a marriage. Most important to us were our feelings and commitment to each other.

We considered the idea of eloping, but when Miranda discussed the idea with her dad, he said he wanted to attend no matter what. So while we would still get married on Maui, we would invite anyone who was willing to join us in taking the long, round-trip journey. While we knew most of our family wouldn't come due to time and money, we wanted to give everyone the opportunity. It was February 2007, and despite wanting to get married in the summer, we postponed our wedding until the following year and informed our families. So with nearly a year and a half to plan such a small wedding, we returned to our daily routines.

While the first two months in Asheville were new and exciting, the excitement was starting to fade. We began doing the same things as back in Cincinnati; a lot of thoughtless routine. We'd exercise, go to work, get home, maybe watch a movie, and then go out to eat on one of our days off.

One night, after another evening of waiting tables, I came home frustrated and fed up with the monotonous routine we had so comfortably succumbed to. I had just ended another shift with the next two days off where we would most likely watch a couple movies, eat dinner somewhere, and then maybe take a hike through the woods. While I may sound spoiled, this life was dull and didn't meet our definition of "ideal". We simply didn't view our time off as a worthwhile reward for our time and effort at work.

"I'm over it," I complained to Miranda. "We work five nights a week to have two days off where we do the same stuff. The mountains are nice, but they're not like the ocean! My job is okay, but it's nothing new. I don't feel like we fit in with the people here who are mainly college students or hippies, and there's no excitement in our lives!"

"I agree," Miranda responded. "So what do you want to do?"

"Who knows? We should just go to the beach. Let's pack some clothes and leave right now." I said jokingly.

"Then let's go," Miranda replied.

"I'm kidding. It's late and we're tired. Let's just go to bed. I'll get over it."

From Mainland to Maui

We had both worked that night, but we wanted the sun, sand and smell of saltwater. We knew how comfortable it would be to stay in our apartment and how uncomfortable it would be to drive overnight to the Atlantic Ocean. I glanced over at our cloud-like mattress blanketed by our down comforter and imagined how wonderful it would feel to go to bed. Then I checked the weather for Myrtle Beach, forecasting sunny and clear days.

"Mir, the weather looks good at Myrtle Beach. Let's go."

At one o'clock in the morning I brewed a pot of coffee and we started packing. It would be inconvenient and uncomfortable driving with no sleep, but the decision to go would drastically change our lives once again.

We were physically exhausted but mentally wide awake as we spontaneously drove to the coast. We didn't know where we would stay once we arrived and never discussed what we would do. We didn't care. We needed to feel the sand and hear the waves, and that's where our thoughts ended.

After driving several hundred miles while drinking coffee, we saw the sun beginning to rise in the distance. Shortly after, we reached our destination. Seeing the water, parking the car, and stepping onto the sand barefoot, we hypnotically walked toward the ocean in silence, witness to one of the most beautiful sights we had ever seen. This wasn't Maui by any means. It wasn't a flawless, world-class beach with clear blue water. This was Myrtle Beach, South Carolina, with trash and cigarette butts littered on the sand, sea gulls using the beach as a toilet, and cold murky water encouraging no one to swim. It was a touristy beach on the Atlantic side of Mainland USA, but gazing at the horizon, I appreciated every second. We were tired, dirty, hungry, and thirsty, but for those few minutes of standing on the beach, we were revived.

While it had been a debate on whether or not abandoning the comforts of home and driving to the beach overnight was worth it, the answer was now clear. It was uncomfortable driving without sleep from the mountains to the sea after a night at work, but uncomfortable things usually have the greatest rewards; and this was no exception. It isn't easy putting forth effort to be temporarily inconvenienced in order to accomplish something you'll later appreciate.

We left the beach and found a spectacular last-minute bargain on a beachfront condo on the 10th floor overlooking the ocean where we could see for miles in the distance. Our time at Myrtle Beach was amazing, making our standard two days off feel like a mini-vacation. We went to an aquarium and touched stingrays for the first time, spent hours circling a lazy river, and spent both days walking up and down the beach having whimsical conversations. We drank margaritas served in "yardsticks" and danced the night away in a club wearing slippers (sandals) before stumbling back to our oceanfront condo. We felt like kids; like we had back on Maui. It was the first time since returning to the Mainland that we had passion, curiosity, and naivety. For the 48 hours we spent on the coast our eyes were open and we were awake. We felt alive and it was incredible.

We sadly left our condo Saturday morning to be back at work that same night. We were ending our mini-vacation, and after the six-hour drive home we would be back to our mindless routines. It was on this solemn drive where we chose to follow our hearts.

7. SUBMITTING TO THE SOUL

As the mountains became visible on the horizon, I thought back to college when I had decided to leave and try something different. Our weekend at the beach had interrupted our routine, giving me a fresh perspective on how I was living. I stopped to think, just like I had during the cigarette break on that gray, cold morning back in Cincinnati.

It began raining as we drove into the mountains with over an hour before we would be home. With every degree the temperature dropped, I became more bitter toward the city we had chosen to call home. The harder it rained, the more I wanted to turn around and go back to the beach. I was once again doing something I didn't want to do, and once again I didn't know why.

I was leaving the beach to drive back "home" where it was cold and wet. While the mountainous city of Asheville was certainly a beautiful place, I felt better near the ocean. I'm not saying the ocean is better than mountains, fields, cities, rivers, or anywhere else; the ocean was simply my preference. We had moved from a place we loved in order to be closer to family, and since moving to Asheville, we'd only seen them once. We were waiting tables for the same pay as in Cincinnati (much less than what we had made on Maui), and we didn't appreciate our days off. While we truly loved being near the ocean, we had chosen to live six hours away from it! This was our reality.

We had left Maui to pursue "The American Dream", and by most standards, we had it good. We owned nice, new stuff and lived extremely comfortably with little stress. We'd get home from work, drink wine by our fireplace, and wake up the next morning to a bedroom window view of snowcapped mountains and ancient pine trees. I drove to work winding through the mountains while pumping Drum and Bass through my car's Bose stereo system. At work, I was one of the head servers and well respected by everyone. Life was good, and to say it wasn't would be a lie. We'd made a successful start in working toward the image we believed to be the best, but it wasn't for us.

After a lengthy discussion driving home in the rain, Miranda and I decided to return to Maui. Despite the effort we would again need to put forth, we believed moving back would make us the happiest. Despite how much money we would lose having just purchased new things now needing resold, despite the distance from our families, and despite the difficulty in purchasing a house on Maui, we were going back. It was where we felt at home and where we wanted to unite in marriage. We had just one problem; we were broke. We had anticipated staying in Asheville for years and had spent all the money we had saved on a car and new furniture. Talk about buyer's remorse just six months later!

Wanting to fly back to Maui as soon as possible, Miranda brought up the money from her inheritance. She hadn't touched it since depositing it into the bank a year ago, but now wanted to use some to move back. I immediately dismissed the idea, knowing how easy it would be to save for another year and then make our return. But Miranda didn't want to wait. Having lost her mom, she had gained a new perspective of life's fragility. Saving money in a place we didn't enjoy didn't make sense and would only prolong what she truly desired. She persuaded me by arguing that we could earn more back on Maui. Then, just like before, we could reimburse ourselves for the moving costs. So it was settled. We would begin ridding ourselves of what we had purchased just six months prior and start re-planning our second move to Maui.

A mental checklist of the many tasks necessary to once again relocate began forming in my head, making me feel sick to my stomach with anxiety. But, for as much as I was nauseous dreading the stressful work, I was equally thrilled.

Rain soaked our clothes as we got home and began pulling our suitcases from the trunk. It had also become much colder but ending our weekend while freezing in the rain didn't bother us at all. We had made the decision to return to where our hearts told us we needed to be. Nothing could have bothered us.

I was in a terrific mood at work that night but decided to keep the news of moving back to Maui to myself, only discussing our weekend on the Atlantic Coast. I would have liked to tell my co-workers, but knowing it could do more harm than good, I kept quiet. Later that night, after a busy Saturday at the restaurant, I came home and dreamt about Hawaii. We were going back, and it couldn't have felt more perfect.

The first part of our seven months in Asheville was spent settling down and getting established, while the last few months were just the opposite. We began planning our move by first talking with the apartment's leasing office and letting them know we'd be breaking our lease. Having never done this sort of thing before, we were both nervous, but it turned out to be much easier and cheaper than expected.

We had scheduled when to move, but now came the more difficult and diminishing task of selling our stuff. This is one of the great challenges people face when moving to Hawaii. They want to move, yet feel such a bond with jobs, houses, cars, and furniture, that they can't. The connection they feel with their stuff (or careers, or societal status) is too great, and if life's success is measured by these things, then to "get ahead" can also mean getting stuck- where the things you own end up owning you. To sell things in order to make significant alterations to life and lifestyle can be nearly impossible if someone has worked hard to obtain success by this definition, and for a lot of people, it's the only thing they've ever pursued. Luckily for us, we had only spent about five months of acquiring before determining we wanted to pursue something different, but it still wasn't easy giving up what things we had.

We too had played the game of working hard to get more, better, faster, and more stylish, but not long enough to become emotionally attached. We would need to sell our expensive mattress with its Egyptian cotton sheets and down comforter, along with our living room set, cars, washer and dryer, and the furniture Miranda had received from her mother. Knowing there would be nothing else given to Miranda by her mom, this could have been hard. Most people would want to keep anything which belonged to a late parent, but she said the furniture and clothes held no sentimental value. She told me that no matter what we owned or where we lived, the memories of her mother would never fade, break, or go away. Her mom was preserved inside, giving little value to physical belongings.

Miranda had no problem with letting go of what would keep us on the Mainland, but I had a difficult time. We worked hard in Cincinnati, and then in Maui waiting tables while staying on a strict budget the entire time. Upon moving to Asheville, I bought some of the nicest things I had ever owned. I wasn't depressed about losing the items; it was the loss of the thousands of dollars that hurt, knowing we could only recover about half of what we had paid for a new mattress and living room set. I also knew I'd be taking a hit on my car which I'd purchased from a dealership.

From Mainland to Maui

This expensive lesson helped me understand why so many people choose to live in situations they dislike. The things that make life so comfortable can also be the very things which prevent us from seeking our dreams. I've never been materialistic but selling what we had so diligently worked for was depressing and frustrating; both financially and emotionally.

We gave our apartment complex two months' notice and planned to keep nothing more than what would fit in my car. So, we began selling everything we could with urgency, preferring to temporarily sleep on the floor rather than be forced to give away our expensive mattress at the last minute.

A couple of weeks prior to leaving Asheville came the uncomfortable time to inform my boss about our plans. Walking into work, I was preparing to tell the proprietor I'd be leaving, but before I could, he stopped me outside.

"David, you've been doing a great job. You're on time, always positive, and I'd love for you to be one of our bartenders," he said smiling with anticipation of my excitement.

I looked down with a sigh, knowing this didn't make my decision to leave any easier. This restaurant had a classy bar which stayed full, making a bartender's job quite lucrative. The position paid the highest hourly wage of anyone in the restaurant, easily exceeding even a manger's salary. I'd shown some interest in becoming a bartender a couple of months prior, but never seriously pursued the position, unlike many of the servers who truly sought after the highly coveted and profitable job.

"I really appreciate that," I said looking at my shoes. "But I'm actually moving back to Maui. I would have loved the position, but unfortunately, this is my official two-week notice to leave."

Upon telling the rest of the crew I was returning to Maui, few were surprised. They had all seen how passionately I described the island, and some thought I was crazy for ever leaving Maui in the first place.

We sold most of our things shortly thereafter, including all of our larger items. It was relieving to see these items sold, but still felt awful losing so much money in such a short amount of time. We donated some of our things to charity, and eventually were forced to give some things to friends who were planning a yard sale. While we had agreed to split whatever money they earned from the sale after we left, we never received a penny from them. With little more than our clothes and a road atlas, we left our apartment. Our plan was to spend time visiting with family and saying goodbyes before flying back to Maui.

It was the middle of August, and our first destination was Florida to visit my older brother and his fiancé. We had no home, no jobs, one car, some clothes, an air mattress, and a road atlas. As we merged on the highway leaving North Carolina, I experienced a freedom I had never before felt-more so than moving to Maui or driving to different cities looking for a place to live. Miranda and I would technically be "homeless", just driving around the Eastern side of the United States visiting with family and sleeping on our air mattress. We had no obligations, no commitments, and no place to be at any certain time. We didn't even have plane tickets to dictate when we would leave for Maui. With our trunk and back seat full of everything we owned, we had a new found feeling of liberty, and leaving our comfortable apartment having sold nearly everything we had acquired, we never looked back. The money we lost and the stuff we sold were never given a thought once they were gone; it was merely the process of losing them that was trying.

Six weeks of traveling quickly flew by. We purchased one-way plane tickets, sold my car, and reserved a vacation rental on Maui for when we arrived. I also reserved a rental car; something we were too young to do when we first moved. We would be making the move again, only this time was different. This time we were going to live our lives rather than vacation for an extended period of time. The first time we moved to Maui we had planned to live there for one year before relocating to a more "livable" city without even considering the possibility of living on Maui permanently. But this time would be different. This time we were letting go and doing what we felt was right for us. We were giving up on the "American Dream" with the two dogs, two kids, big house, stable careers, and two weeks per year to splurge on an elaborate vacation. We understood that we might never own a house or become rich, but that we could live richly by having a simple life catered to our own preferences. We were surrendering to our dream and achieving success by our own definition.

8. THE PLEASANT REALITY OF SUCCESS REDEFINED

Returning to Maui felt as natural and reviving as waking up after a good night's sleep. Having been off the island for just under a year, we were instantly greeted by the floral scented airport I had so vividly remembered. We were home.

Postponing our strong desire to vacation, we quickly bought a car and found a place to live. Our condo was a small (450 sq. ft.) studio, furnished with a full-size bed, an old TV displaying only three-quarters of the screen, and a sofa. While it was only one room, the unit was relatively inexpensive and newly remodeled. The complex also had a tennis court, pool, and hot tub. But what we enjoyed most was the view looking from our lanai; past the tennis court, across the street, through the park, and under some trees for a glimpse of the ocean. It wasn't always comfortable sharing a small bed; we couldn't have company and didn't have a large enough kitchen to make a complete dinner. But for us, seeing the sunlight dancing on the water and the big sky over the community tennis court made it all worthwhile.

It was the beginning of November, and from July (when we decided to move back to Maui) until now, we'd been extremely busy. Selling our stuff, leaving Asheville, visiting with family across several states, flying back to Maui, rushing to buy a car, and then moving left us exhausted. It was time to treat ourselves to a few weeks of vacationing. We wouldn't be eating out, going to luaus, and paying for excursions, but we didn't need to. To fill days and weeks with those kinds of things can even take away from the experience of being on Maui all-together.

During our time off we lived simply and in a state of appreciation. Without much we "had to do", we were able to take the time to enjoy the little things in life. We determined what we wanted (which was lounging on the beach), then enjoyed our choice. While working, paying bills, running errands, shopping, studying, and everything else, it's easy to live hurriedly while neglecting life's journey and taking it for granted.

The first month back was our chance to relax, and for a while, it was wonderful. Our days consisted of waking up and casually brewing a pot of coffee before eating breakfast on our lanai. We talked about which beach to visit and then got started. Our "nine to five" was spent in the sand. Everyday we'd pack a lunch and drive to one of our favorite beaches with chairs, an umbrella, books, snorkel sets, and body boards. We were in our early twenties and living the life most people envision of vacationing or retiring in Hawaii. While our old high school classmates worked on reports and syllabi, we worked on our tan. While many people sat in a florescent-lit office building, we sat marveling at another glorious sunset. Once the sun fell into the ocean, we'd go home, have dinner, and watch some TV or soak in the hot tub before going to bed. This was our routine, day in and day out.

After a couple weeks of beach-bumming, I made some interesting observations. First, I noticed how much time we saved making food a small priority. We rarely cooked, rarely ate dinner at our table, and viewed eating like brushing our teeth or getting a shower; it was just something we needed to do. So we ate microwavable meals, lunchmeat sandwiches, and cereal. Not caring about what, when, where, and how we ate saved a lot of time and money. The second thing I came to find in this time of melting the day away in the sun was how quickly it became old. We stopped going to the beach as often and started taking our situation for granted. When we had first lived on Maui, we worked five days a week and lived every day to the fullest. So now, having grown tired of our carefree, unproductive routine, it was time to find a job.

Before we had a chance to look at any "help wanted" ads, a storm came. Not just any storm, but a saturating tropical storm like we had never experienced. We woke up the next morning to flooded roads and a power outage that would last for nearly 48 hours. Kihei's main road was a river of water, mud, and overflowing sewers, trapping us inside for an evening of playing cards by flashlight. The next morning, we shopped for breakfast in the grocery store, again by flashlight, and spent an entire hour driving the one mile home in nightmarish traffic. After a week of shoveling mud out of the streets and driveways, things were back to normal and we were on the job hunt.

We finally saw an ad hiring for a restaurant right on the beach. Applying in person dressed in some of the nicest clothes we owned, we were hired on the spot. Not only had we landed the first job we applied for, but we would also be working together in an oceanfront restaurant with one of the best views on Maui.

We expected a call the next day to hear when we would start, but the call never came. The management said they would call, but they didn't on that day, or the next day, or the next. So we gave up on the beachfront restaurant and applied elsewhere before finally receiving the call we had so anxiously awaited. This sort of thing (taking a long time to do anything) is commonplace on Maui, and when finally getting the call, we were asked to start that day! Completely unprepared, we told them we needed to buy some clothes and could start the following afternoon.

From Mainland to Maui

Entering the restaurant the next day and bearing witness to the spectacular panoramic ocean view was breathtaking. After meeting a manager and filling out paperwork, we watched the line of people who had been waiting at the door begin flooding into the dining room. With just two days until Christmas, the island was full of tourists excited to celebrate the holidays. To our surprise, our first night was the busiest evening the restaurant had seen all year.

We spent Christmas away from our families for the first time ever, and while this time of year was difficult for some of our co-workers, we didn't mind. The previous Christmas had been difficult for more reasons than one, and we didn't have time to dwell on being thousands of miles away; we were hard at work. The sunny beachside Christmas Day dinner of turkey and stuffing quickly passed, and days later we were back at work watching fireworks over the ocean to bring in the New Year.

A couple months later, we were accustomed to our jobs, enjoying a steady routine, and back to living similar to the way we had before; but this time was different. I can't say whether it was better or worse, just different. The fantasy island we had fallen in love with now felt commonplace. I was told from someone who had lived on Maui for several years that it was just like living anywhere else and the only difference was that you have more options all year-round. You don't always need to hike, go to the beach or enjoy the outdoors, but you always have the option. Maui had become merely a place to live, only with better weather, nicer scenery, friendlier people, and a more laid-back lifestyle. Being surrounded by nature, Maui was nature, and our life on Maui felt natural.

It was February, and with the intention of getting married in June, now was the time to start planning our wedding. We picked the date, sent out invitations, selected a cake, and hired a photographer. After viewing numerous breathtaking spots on Maui, we decided to get married on the beach in front of where we worked, and then have our reception in the restaurant. We sent invitations to our entire family, despite knowing the majority would not attend, and eventually received RSVPs from fifteen of our closest family members and two of our best friends from Cincinnati who said they would come. We told them to bring only themselves and to save the toaster ovens and bath towels for wedding couples who needed them. We just wanted to see our family at our wedding and for them to see our island home. To have our family on Maui meant more to us than the biggest wedding registry I could imagine.

Our friends and family arrived months later with some time to visit before the wedding, allowing us to play "tour guide" for a few days. We had arranged for the group to meet the night before the ceremony at an ocean side park in Kihei. We considered taking everyone to a restaurant for something more "proper", but what was the point? There was no rehearsal, and how great is a lunchmeat sandwich at the park while watching a Hawaiian sunset?! We could have eaten at a restaurant, but our picnic was perfect. It was a way for everyone to meet prior to our upcoming ceremony the next morning and concluded with a glorious sunset.

It was another beautiful morning on Maui, perfect for our nine o'clock wedding. Miranda looked stunning as she walked onto the sand in her elegant white gown. The ceremony (officiated by Miranda's grandfather) was magnificent. Purple leis hung from the necks of our seventeen witnesses as they stood on the beach facing us with the ocean our background, accompanied by a solo harpist off to the side. The harpist played softly near a special lei hanging from a stake we had placed in the sand, symbolizing the presence of Miranda's mother.

From Mainland to Maui

Following the understated and casual reception for brunch, Miranda and I drove to the Four Seasons Resort for the nicest hotel stay we'd ever experienced. We savored dinner at the resort's steakhouse that night and slept like boulders. The wait was over. The hard work and planning had come to an end. We were starting our marriage the next morning with a flight to Seattle for an Alaskan cruise.

Another serene Maui morning greeted our honeymoon as our valet attendant bid us farewell with chilled bottles of water. The week spent in Alaska can only be described as magical, and while ending the most elaborate trip we'd ever taken was somewhat depressing, the feeling of returning home to Maui was amazing. We had lived on Maui for almost two years and this was the first time we'd vacationed to return to our home on Maui. It's quite spectacular coming home to your favorite place in the world.

Following our honeymoon, the start of our marriage was horrendous. Not as a result of our relationship, but from the tremendous changes we immediately made after we wed. In our first month as husband and wife, we moved into an unfurnished condo with a bedroom for more space, we both quit smoking cigarettes, and Miranda changed jobs. She was hired as a cart attendant on a golf course, and the time change was trying. She'd wake up at 5:30 A.M. and leave at 6:30 A.M. while I stayed in bed having worked the night before. She would then get home at 4 P.M., just after I left for work, and we would not see each other until she was ready for bed. Sometimes she would already be asleep on the couch before I came home. We'd always have the same two days off, but during the week, we rarely saw each other.

Four months passed of working opposite hours and living in a dark condo that felt nothing like home. During this time, Miranda was put on antidepressants. Sudden changes can induce clinical depression, and within 45 days the following had occurred: we married, took time off work, enjoyed an extravagant honeymoon, immediately moved into an unfurnished condo while owning no furniture, and quit smoking cigarettes. Between moving, chewing nicotine gum and shopping for furniture, Miranda also started a new job in a different field working opposite hours to what we were accustomed.

Something had to give. We both agreed we could no longer work separate shifts and that one of us needed to change jobs. I was still at the beachfront restaurant making good money and having a great time in the process. Miranda, on the other hand, was uncertain about her job. We decided to give it some time, waiting to see if she wanted to continue working on the course. In the meantime, we wanted to move to a place which would allow us to have a dog.

Two months later, we happily moved into a two-bedroom condo in South Kihei. Our unit was on the top floor of a quiet building with lots of sunlight, a breeze from the mountains, and views of the ocean and Haleakala. We each had our own bathroom, a 2nd bedroom we used as an office and a remodeled kitchen with new appliances. Then we found our puppy; a playful and energetic three-month-old Japanese Spitz.

Life improved with the responsibility and companionship of raising a puppy, especially for Miranda who had taken herself off her antidepressants and was suffering from withdrawal. While it's recommended to wean off this medication, Miranda did not, and after learning more about the drugs, threw her remaining supply in the trash.

Continuing to work opposite shifts brought us to the point where neither of us wanted to work. We started viewing life as hard work that reaped little reward. That's when I decided to write this book. The idea had started more than a year earlier as I was walking by the ocean in the same park that we had picnicked the night before our wedding. I

From Mainland to Maui

had walked the shore of that park many times, but this day I slowed down. As I leisurely strolled in solitude a few hours before work, I noticed some stairs descending into the ocean. I decided to take a seat on this new discovery to spend a few minutes gazing out at the horizon. Looking over at the island of Lana'i, I thought about my life, comparing my past and present, and in that moment, I felt blessed. My life had greatly improved to be relaxing in Hawaii on a lovely day before my five hour shift at work.

I then thought about how my life could improve. I thought about the future and thought about what I viewed to be worth pursuing. I thought about what I was doing with my time; in my blessed life of working 20 hours a week with enough money to comfortably sleep, eat, and shower after a day at the beach. We lived simply and didn't have much, but I didn't want much. I was happy with our island home, what I was doing for work, my wife, our dog, and the things we had. I didn't want anything more, so I felt no reason to be better. Nothing other than what we were already doing seemed worth my time and effort. I had no motivation. I had no reason to earn more, learn more, or find my full potential. Nothing seemed worth pursuing, and it was sad.

Then I thought about others. Our lives were great, but what about my family? What about our friends, the people we had met and the millions of people suffering from a defeated mentality? While I was enjoying the sun and the breeze, I thought about the many people spending most of their time doing things they'd rather not. I thought about the people who believed they would never see exotic places and never have a chance to watch their dreams evolve. I thought about you, and the possibility that you may never experience what it feels like to live every minute of every day in appreciation of the choices you make. Encouraging others to discover and pursue their dreams was my driver; this book is a result.

Miranda and I were at our boiling point with working opposite hours when I decided to quit my job and write. It wasn't easy leaving the oceanfront restaurant knowing I would no longer be producing an income. I give Miranda credit for helping me lower my priority of money and understanding that helping people find happiness is something that goes beyond a bank account. So I started writing. After waking up with Miranda and seeing her off to work, I would sit down at my computer. Being on the same schedule improved everything, and before long, Miranda had the anti-depressants out of her system and life was beautiful. We spent every evening together (a first in our entire relationship given our previous restaurant hours), and for the first time felt as if we had a proper place to call home. We had our own furniture and put great effort into decorating and personalizing the condo. We took our dog for walks on the beach, watched the sun setting across the ocean from our lanai, and watched the sun rising behind Haleakala every morning. For the first time in our lives we lived slowly and with no plans of moving or making any significant changes in our newly-wed life. Then the phone rang.

I had just stepped in from a morning jog while Miranda had woken up with a migraine and was lying on the couch. It was our landlord telling us he had sold his house and would be moving back into his (our) condo. We needed to move out and find a new place to live.

It was a frustrating month trying to find a place that would feel like home and also allow pets. One day we saw a sign in the front yard of a large oceanfront house. Miranda and I were both tired and discouraged having just spent hours looking at condos and ohanas with no luck. She told me not to even bother with calling the number, knowing the house would cost way more than we could afford, but I decided to call anyway. After leaving a message and getting a callback, I was told the house was indeed over our budget. However, the owner said she would also be renting an ohana currently being remodeled which too was oceanfront. She said it was small and currently in horrible shape due to the remodel, but that it would soon be available.

Getting off the phone and imagining the two of us living in an oceanfront ohana had me speechless. Then we saw it a week later. As the owner walked us through the small ohana under construction, all I could do was look outside. Inside was a mess, but we didn't care. If we rented this place, every morning we would wake up right next to the ocean and see Lana'i light up pink as the sun rose. Every night we could watch the sun melt into the ocean, signaling the end of another day in paradise. We truly desired the seaside spot, and after praying and waiting, we were blessed. We would unimaginably live in an oceanfront home.

We never had a chance to see how beautifully the remodel would turn out before we moved in, but we didn't care about being first time users of a new bathroom and kitchen; that was just a bonus. We would have paid good money to pitch a tent on the lawn. We signed a lease on the same day we saw the finished product, and it was impressive. The ohana was impeccable and spotlessly clean.

Once every box was piled inside, I stepped out the living room door. I was miles from reality watching the sun slowly fall into the ocean's horizon from my own backyard. It was surreal. It was a dream. I'd always pictured movie stars and pop singers occupying the oceanfront spots in Hawaii; never me at the age of 24.

I now awake to waves crashing outside my bedroom/lanai screen door. The soft chirping of birds is gently drowned out by the sound of rolling water pulling pebbles into the sea before tossing them back. Raising my heavy eyelids, I glance out my sliding glass door to see the water. The clouds and islands visible in the distance are shades of fuchsia, painted by the sun rising behind Haleakala. Looking at the silvery surface of the

David J. Gross

placid ocean and crawling out of bed, I spot a turtle poking his head out to take a breath. Walking into the kitchen, I pour a cup of Kona coffee, adding a teaspoon of cane sugar to the scheduled brew. Finding it impossible to look away from the ocean just steps away, I hypnotically walk across my backyard to the stairs leading into the water. The air feels cool as the tropics wait to be warmed by the sun. My day is now started and I feel alive.

This is my life now and it's no longer a dream. I accepted that I was unhappy with my life, where I lived, and what I was doing. I think a lot of us want different, I just had the courage to admit my desire and go for it. I discovered what I deemed worth my time and effort and made it my first priority. I went for my dream, despite its concerns, despite its uncertainties, and despite its demands. I realized I was playing a game I didn't find fun, for I didn't want money, a college degree, and nice material things. I wanted to live, feel alive, and just be. I wanted to be happy. I wanted to live in appreciation every moment and be mentally present; in the present. If I were perfect, I could do that anywhere in the world, but I'm not. I admittedly lose sight of the good things in life, but Maui is always there to refocus my vision.

So today, after many years of believing I knew what was worth my time and effort, I admit I was wrong. I was pursuing someone else's dream, and my dream was different; not better, just different. If after reading this you also want to move to Maui, do reconsider, because it's potentially not your authentic personal desire. But you do have one. Everyone has a dream, and everyone can bring greatness to their life, leaving a legacy that says, "I did exactly what I deemed to be worth my time and energy". Will you?

PART TWO

S. Stop Everything

Stop (v.)- To come to a stand, as in a course or journey

Life Can't Stop, Only You Can

There are four things necessary before anything can be pursued; stop, think, observe, and plan. While taking four actions before trying something may sound unreasonable, think about it. Whether you're running for public office or using the toilet, you need to do those four things. If you're sitting on the couch watching a football game and nature calls, what's the first thing you need to do? Stop. Unless you have a TV in your bathroom or a toilet in your living room, you have to temporarily stop watching the football game.

Stopping is the first action toward achieving success; however, this is not easy. It's why so many people fail to lose weight, fail to quit smoking, complain about work, gripe about the weather, become angry with their spouse, and frustrated with traffic. It's not impossible to stop, although it may sometimes feel that way, but it does require patience, time, and a willingness to temporarily break away from the fast-paced life to which we've grown accustomed.

If you're a woman, while you may be more impatient than you should be, you're probably better than most men when it comes to preparing and planning. Women in general are more thoughtful and patient than men. Men buy things needing assembly and want to put it together before reading the instructions, and instead of stopping to ask for directions, we just want to drive faster. To stop means to hinder, discontinue, put an end to, and to prevent from proceeding. So why should we slow down or stop when slowing down only prolongs the rewards our efforts obtain? Because it's possible our lives are not going in the right direction and heading to places where we don't want to go.

Picture Joe Schmoe waking up on a Saturday morning near the beginning of fall. It's a beautiful day, with clear skies, cool temperatures, warm sun, and great weather forecasted for the entire weekend. Monday's a holiday, and Joe the electrician doesn't need to be back to work until Tuesday, so he packs up the car, eager to enjoy his three-day weekend. He's booked a cabin by a lake for three days of boating, fishing, and relaxing in the wilderness. Having been given directions to the lake over the phone while making the cabin reservation, he hops in the car and starts driving. To stop or even slow down would only delay him from arriving to kick his feet up and sip a cold brew while overlooking the lake. The problem (at least potentially) is that he's driving and putting all his faith in the directions he was given over the phone. All his efforts in racing to get to the lake are solely reliant on someone he spoke with. Having never looked at a map himself, Joe can only hope this person knew how to get there and accurately explained the route.

Today you're Joe driving that car. Your cabin by the lake may be retirement, graduation, or a million dollars in the bank. It may be a vacation, the weekend, or what we call a "pau hana" in Hawaii (an after-work cocktail). Unfortunately, if you're like most people, you haven't stopped to look at your own life's map for directions. Instead, you've been traveling using only the directions you were given. The people giving the directions may have been your parents, teachers, peers, employers, society, or even government officials; and the directions they've given are very similar or identical to the directions they were once given. Without investigating for ourselves, how can we know if these directions are accurate?

Few people actually look at their own map and draw their individual route. It's easier for us to get directions over the phone than to sit down and do the work for ourselves. We assume that if someone else has already been there, we should save ourselves the hassle by listening to them. Making this assumption, or any assumption for that matter, creates serious problems.

By now it's too late to start at the beginning. We're en route. We've taken directions from other people and have most likely become lost along the way. To make matters worse, even if the directions are perfect, the cabin by the lake may fall short of our expectations. Do we even want to pursue the cabin by the lake? Would we prefer to go to the mountains, or to the ocean, or somewhere else? Are we driving in the right direction, to the right place, and in the best way?

Today I'm asking you to stop, despite how difficult it may be, and get new directions. Stop moving, figure out what you want, and map your route. Slowing down and coming to a complete stop is one of the hardest things in the world for us to do, as we've been told to gain more, get better, and move faster. It's not something that comes naturally and stopping takes concentration. However, time is irreplaceable, and we need to stop and think about life and what's worth doing while we still have the chance.

If you get lost in the middle of the woods and find yourself in a survival situation, the first step is to stop. It would be easy to panic while lost in the woods, especially if it's cold or uncomfortable, and you could run around trying to find the path you wandered off, potentially dying in the process. Many of us panic in our lives, especially when things become uncomfortable. You may be unemployed or losing your house and panicking to find a job. You may be failing a class or losing a relationship, and in all these situations it can be instinctive to rush out and try to fix things without giving much thought. But taking action before stopping to think can leave us in worse shape than when we started.

If you're unemployed, you could scramble to find a job, despite the nature of the work or ethical issues it may create. In school, you could take drugs to help you study, or cheat on a test for a better grade. You may have recently ended a relationship with a significant other, only to create a bad situation with a "rebound". Maybe you are altogether struggling with life, finding it of little value and with no excitement; like there is no point to getting out of bed. If this is the case, it can be easy to get into a lot of trouble rushing to find excitement and seeking worth. While it's not easy, especially in bad situations, stop what you are doing before taking action.

When I say stop, I'm not saying to quit your job or to stop making house payments. I mean to physically stop at some part in your day and mentally relax. When's the last time you've done it; really stopped everything? Not sitting on the couch and watching TV or lying down to take a nap. Not taking a week away from your job to work on the house or putting a movie on pause. Being honest and giving this question thought, when's the last time you've completely stopped?

You may not be able to remember the last time you've stopped, so try it in the middle of your day. Don't listen to music, watch TV, eat, sleep, or think about your plans for the weekend. Just stop. Taking a minute to "smell the roses" can help wake us up and question whether we've been living like zombies.

The Zombie Analogy

What are zombies? Obviously, they're fictional and make for a good horror flick, but what are some characteristics of them and why do people defend against them? If you get bit by a zombie, you'll become one yourself. But what's so wrong with becoming a zombie? They have a decent life. They always have a large group of like-minded friends who boycott fashion, never seem hurried, and never feel pain. You could shoot off an arm and they'd still be moseying along in a mindless stupor, unconcerned by the blood loss and missing limb. Their whole purpose and goal in life is to bite healthy people and convert them into zombies. They want to multiply. With a basic goal, many friends, and a continual Morphine high, the life of a zombie doesn't sound too bad. What do you think?

How about for the "good guys", the humans, what do their lives look like? Well, in the movies, they're usually terrified and working very hard to stay alive. It's not the zombies who are suffering, but the humans. We're the panicked ones on screen, wildly running around and screaming for our lives. It would certainly be easier to submissively lie down and let one of the "dead souls" bite you versus the alternative. And choosing this route would be a choice, eliminating both fear and the constant struggle of staying alive.

Choosing to become a lifeless zombie could be ideal, but in the movies there's usually only one of three outcomes. The first possibility is that humanity wins by defeating the zombies and goes on to live happily ever after repopulating the planet. That typically doesn't happen. Zombies most often take over the planet, and because no one has food, everyone dies and the world ends. The third possibility of what happens at the end of these grotesque films is that the humans isolate themselves and search for a cure. These "survivors" understand that until a cure is found, conscious humans and mind-dead zombies can never live together.

When stopping to look around, you can see how America is full of zombies- full of people who don't think. Many of us go through the motions of daily life hurried, performing monotonous chores which reap mediocre rewards. More and more people are choosing to be sucked into a culture that promotes comfort and discourages taking risks; a culture we've been told is ideal. More and more people are choosing to lie down and get bit, extinguishing fear and doubt from their life and consequentially rejecting the ability to live as they choose.

The movie of your life will end at some point. Will you give up, or fight to stay alive? While it's easier to live like a zombie, if we all choose to suppress our dreams, how will anyone survive?

Sleepwalking Through Routine

Have you ever heard someone say, "I've done it so much I could do it in my sleep?" If you're like most, you have a lot of structure and scheduling in your life. You go to work or school at a certain time each morning, leave around the same time in the afternoon, and have the same drive to and from these places. You most likely go to bed around the same time and wake up in the same bed and by the same sound of the same alarm clock. You drink the same brand of coffee, go to the same websites, watch the same television shows, and read the same newspaper. You do pretty much the same things on the weekend with little variety- eating at one of the five restaurants you frequent and going to the same stores for the same items. Could you be living your life in your sleep?

Another well used phrase is, "I know it like the back of my hand", but have you ever really looked at the back of your hand? When I first asked myself that question, I honestly had to answer with no. I've never truly examined the back of my hand. I've never stopped to give attention and conscious thought to what the back of my hand really looks like. However, I have seen the back of my hands many times and can even picture them in my mind.

There are many things in life that are like the back of our hand. Do you know your drive to work like the back of your hand? Perhaps your day at work, time in school, morning routine, dinner at night, or time on the weekend you know quite well, yet don't give these moments attention. What things in your life do you "know like the back of your hand"?

Routines performed without thought can prevent us from living and have the potential to make us feel like we're sleepwalking through life. With so much of the same, life can feel like one big déjà vu. These thoughtless days can pass without any lasting reward, just filled with tasks to make life more comfortable.

However, routines and schedules can be wonderful if used properly. I personally plan my days in advance and can better focus when setting aside specific times for specific things. Routines can sometimes even be imperative to finding success but can also lead to a life of thoughtless monotony.

Our Four Needs

Everything we have in life has needs to maintain their purpose. Our bodies need food and water, a toilet needs to be cleaned and repaired, a car needs gas and maintenance, and even shoes need cleaned and polished. Basic needs are demanding and can occupy a lot of time and energy. However, when looking at the definition of the word "need", a necessary duty or obligation, we see that we don't have too many needs at all. What we have are choices.

Sometimes I get hungry while writing and need to stop to eat. Realistically, I don't need to eat, and could survive for days without food. But I do need to eat if I don't want a headache. I choose to eat because I don't want a headache or the feeling of hunger. So, while eating was not required for survival, I did need to eat to maintain my current headache-free, healthy status.

I believe that when looking at all the things that occupy our time, we have four kinds of needs; survival needs, relative needs, integrity needs, and legacy needs. Everything we do fits into these four categories. I've put them in order from the most basic and commonly satisfied, to the most complex, frequently misunderstood, and undervalued. It's this rarely pursued, yet highly rewarding need required for true success; the need to fulfill your own personal legacy.

Survival Needs

The first and most basic of our four needs pertain to survival. Every living thing requires food, water, and protection from the elements. Whether you're a human, an elephant, a beetle, a fish, or a shrub, without these three things, life is impossible. Speaking in approximations, we, as humans, can survive without water for 3-4 days and 3-4 weeks without food. Protection from the elements has many variables, with the most important and ever-present being the temperature. With hyperthermia and hypothermia being two of the greatest threats of the outdoors, regulating our body's core temperature of 98.6 degrees Fahrenheit is essential. If you're in North Dakota in February, you either need to be somewhere inside, somewhere by a fire, or wearing warm clothes to protect you from the cold. If you're in the desert in the middle of summer, you could burn in no time. If you're in Hawaii, no worries; enjoy the 70's and 80's, stay in the shade, and enjoy the trades.

From Mainland to Maui

While temperature is the most prevalent factor in surviving the elements, there are plenty of life-threatening natural occurrences as well. Things like hurricanes, earthquakes, tsunamis, and avalanches are just a few. However, the humbling truth is that no matter how much we prepare for these events, there's little we can do for protection. I've done what little I can to prepare for a disaster, such as a hurricane, yet give little thought to the possibility. I understand my vulnerability and worrying about what may or may not occur does nothing to improve my life.

While food, water, and shelter are the only things needed to keep us (our bodies) alive, everything has individual and specific needs. Let's say a beauty pageant contestant was seen and photographed doing drugs. I would think that her beauty pageant career just died. Therefore, a need for her to continue competing in pageants would be to refrain from doing drugs; or at least not get caught.

Everything in life has needs to maintain its current status. Jobs, cars, houses, boats, roads, computers, and everything else will not survive without maintenance. If you don't change the oil of your car, the running capability will slowly die. If you never replace the roof on a house it will eventually leak and lose its status of being a solid, water-resistant building. Computers need upgraded to stay efficient and roads need maintained to serve their purpose. Even a pencil needs sharpened to keep its ability to write. Everything has needs. Keeping this in mind, let's look at relative needs, which frequently occupy much of our time.

Relative Needs

As the mother and daughter roamed the store, Cindy sees something her friend has, "Mommy, Rachel's got one. I have to get one too! I'll die without one!" Though this may sound absurd, there is some truth in this child's statement. While Cindy won't literally keel over and die if she doesn't get what Rachel has, something is affected.

Everyone participates in the game of relative needs to some degree, and the older we get, the more our relative needs increase. As the people we meet, experiences we have, and things we possess all multiply, so do these needs. There are many forms of relative needs in all areas of life. In the business field, relative needs can be beneficial by improving efficiency and lowering consumer cost by creating competition. However, this competition can be expensive and timely.

Let's pretend Sally is in the competitive field of real estate sales. She strives to be the best and is always looking for a competitive edge. Every real estate agent in the area has a laptop computer, but Sally's has built-in wireless internet. She can work online in many locations instead of being limited to the office. It's a wonderful tool that gives her a competitive edge in her field.

One day, another sales agent (Jane) comes into the office showcasing her new laptop which connects to the internet via satellite. She's now moved from the home or office, to anywhere! Now, any time Jane gets an e-mail, she can simply pull her car to the side of the road and respond immediately; great for her, not so great for Sally. Sally is now technologically behind, relative to Jane (the competition). For Sally to stay competitive, she needs the same level of communication, if not better, so Sally races to the store and buys a new laptop. This new computer was a relative need, relative to that of the other sales agent's computer.

Two months go by and another agent (Fred) comes in with a cell phone that stays connected to the internet wherever he goes. He can also connect a headset, making him even more efficient. Looks like it's time for Sally to go back to the store!

This is one example of the never ending game of relative needs. It's a non-stop cycle, and, if occupying too much time, can be detrimental to success. Competition is something that's made America one of the most prosperous countries in the world. It encourages us to challenge ourselves, promotes innovation, and results in greater efficiency. However, when competing in relative needs becomes our sole purpose in life, it leaves no time for anything else. With everything continually becoming more complex, competing in every area of life is impossible. We'll not only go broke, both financially and chronologically, but will also be perpetually exhausted.

So, in what should we compete? We should compete in whatever we choose, understanding the choice can only be made by the individual and no one else. In what do you compete? How much time do you spend on relative needs? Is everything you own and everything you do worth the time and effort?

When giving effort toward any relative need, we have to ask ourselves what is gained. For the real estate agent, the competitive edge was desired for more money, more sales, or the fulfillment of a personal goal. If it's a competitive challenge driven by the desire to fulfill a dream, great! But if it's the money or sales, you have to ask what they're trying to keep alive. What is the need that requires more money or sales?

Let's look at what Sally could be trying to maintain. If Sally's monthly mortgage payment was $2,000, she needs to make at least $24,000 a year just to keep her home ownership alive. That's justifiable if she truly values her home, but what if she doesn't? She could be leasing a fancy sports car and needs the money to make the payments. She could be saving up to travel the world, and if she stops, her dream of traveling could die.

It's possible that what Sally is trying to acquire or maintain isn't an item at all, but a status or title. Sometimes, people just want a gold-plated nametag that says, "Hello, my name is (blank), and I'm a (blank)". These labels can look good, but the longer they're worn, the more inseparable they become. If you're a top-selling real estate agent, that's what you are and how you're perceived by others. To forfeit certain labels and statuses can be more difficult than the effort it took to achieve them in the first place. What it takes to maintain the image we present to others can frequently be assumed as worthwhile without ever giving it thought.

While the competition for relative needs obviously exists in the business world, it also applies to many, if not all, areas of life. When stopping to think, every aspect of life is a competition which can deceive us into believing things are different than they truly are. When looking at things as relative (something we do without thought), we're forced to categorize and label using comparisons rather than allowing ourselves to be objectively honest. We have grown up to compare and compete, and always view things as relative, rather than just what they are.

Playstation can be a lot of fun until you play the newest Playstation 3, making the original Playstation seem dull, unrealistic, and old. The brand-new Honda Civic from the factory line isn't nearly as nice a year later when it's no longer the newest. Twenty years ago, a 1,500 square foot house would be considered a good size. Have you seen some of the new houses today?!

As we compete, we continue getting bigger, better, and faster, increasing the standard and relative needs. You need more time and materials to put a roof on a 6,000 square foot house versus one a quarter of its size. More materials for the house require more money and labor. You need better technology for cars or video games, and more farmland to satisfy bigger appetites. Better technology requires more schooling, and more farming requires more tools. Better requires better, and more requires more.

Relative needs exist everywhere; home, school, work, church, camp, and parties. In high school, clothing is more than just a way to keep warm or a means to cover up. If you have the newest styles and brand names, you're viewed and treated differently than someone wearing thrift store hand-me-downs. Is the relative need for nicer clothes worth the time and effort it takes to obtain and maintain them?

We, as Americans, compete in everything! Jobs, houses, cars, clothes, income, appearance, education, televisions, music players, cell phones, vacations, and even the gifts we give to other people have all become competitions, relative to our fellow Americans. But, if we compete in all of these areas, how much time will we have for anything else? How much effort, money, time, and energy do we spend pursuing what others have? Is it worth competing in all these categories?

We need to consciously choose what we value and commit our time to while determining for ourselves what is worthwhile. When deciding (deciding is the key) to compete in anything, we must understand and accept feeding the needs they require. This is never-ending, for what is applauded as a winner today will be deemed a loser tomorrow. This is the game of relative needs, and it takes continual time and effort.

In what do you compete? What do you find worth your time and effort, and what do you want to eliminate? What would you do with extra time, energy, and money?

Integrity Needs

While relative needs involve others, integrity needs are individual. Everyone is different in many ways, but all similar in this respect- we all have common sense and a feeling of what's right. If you do something that makes you feel guilty, you have compromised your integrity, and if you do something you feel is wrong, everything else will be affected.

There's debate between whether we are born with a "moral code", or if this knowledge of ethics is something that's learned. This is irrelevant. We all know (one way or another) what's wrong and right, and to do something unethical is detrimental to success.

Fortunately, to satisfy this need doesn't take much time. Satisfying integrity needs is usually just not doing what we know we shouldn't. Doing the right thing isn't always viewed as a need and is oftentimes overlooked in our quest for success. However, to be successful in whatever you're pursuing, upholding your integrity is imperative. This is why you hear stories of wealthy, "successful" people committing suicide or abusing drugs and alcohol. While they may appear happy, they have internal guilt and regret about how they are living. Therefore, in whatever we pursue, it must be done with a clean conscience, and without harming the freedoms and choices of others.

Legacy Needs

The last need is what this book is all about. Legacy needs vary greatly, are completely different for each individual, and are required to fulfill our potential. Regretfully, satisfying the desire to do something extraordinary is commonly overlooked and/or evaded. The appeal to shy away from this need is great, as pursuing a legacy is usually hard, always uncomfortable, and can be dangerous. It's not required for survival but is inconceivably necessary to truly live.

From Mainland to Maui

I personally have identified and had the courage to pursue two legacy needs in my life. The first was leaving college to work full time while saving money to move to Maui. The second was to quit my job and write this book. Legacy needs are completely different for everyone and take time to identify. They are the things in life that make us say, "I have to do it, for if I don't, I won't be able to live with myself."

You're most likely in one of two categories. In the first group are those who are certain of their dreams without a shadow of a doubt. You could be a 42-year-old restaurant manager who wants to become an astronaut or an 18-year-old preparing for college who really wants to pursue acting. You could be someone who wants to climb Mt. Everest or work to find a cure for cancer. If you're in the second category, your dreams have been lost or forgotten by spending too much time and effort on life's other needs. How can this change? How can you begin to uncover that which will bring passion, excitement, and fulfillment to life?

If survival needs are not fulfilled, your body will die. If relative needs are not met, an image, status, comfort, luxury, convenience, or title dies. By ignoring integrity needs and not doing what you know to be right, self-esteem and self-respect are damaged. But by shying away from legacy needs, you have driven a stake through the heart of your dreams and killed the one thing you have for potential success. It's what takes your life from mediocrity and transforms it into a wonderfully exciting new world. It's your dream, your goal, and what gives you identity. Even animals satisfy the first three needs and are arguably better than we humans at all of them.

When looking at America today, everyone works to survive, nearly everyone competes for relative needs, many people try doing the right thing, but just a small percentage actually put effort toward their personal passion. If you're one of the brave souls with the courage to pursue this legacy need, great! But before getting started, you need to have time. Stop to consider how you can spend more time on lasting, legacy-creating goals, and less time on relative needs. While it may seem like the clock is an enemy, stop to realize what you truly appreciate, then give less priority to what you don't value.

Not too long ago, people needed to work nearly all day long, all year long, just to satisfy survival needs. People often died because they couldn't stay warm, didn't have basic medicines, or couldn't get enough food and water. Times have changed! For the majority of us in America, we don't need to struggle to stay alive. This leaves a lot of time for other things. Sadly, many of us get so wrapped up in what to wear, what cell phone to buy, and what car to drive, that we flood our schedules with maintaining these comforts. Do we really value these things? What could we do without? What things do we have, and what takes so much of our time? A good way to answer these questions is to imagine your life with nothing.

Getting to Zero

In order to become aware of what occupies your time, resources, money and efforts, visualize your life with nothing. To mentally portray our lives with absolutely nothing is difficult as we've become so accustomed to the way things are, with the many luxuries, comforts and conveniences of this modern world. It takes concentration, but it can help you see the needs you have, then determine what needs you want to have. I know that sounds like an oxymoron, and it is, but we frequently confuse wants with needs.

Certain comforts in life we can't even recognize, and no longer even view as luxuries. Take hot running water for example. This is not something we consciously think about and consciously appreciate having, but years ago, and in some parts of the world today, this common convenience couldn't even be imagined. Reflecting on your own conveniences can help identify what you appreciate so you can eliminate those you don't.

Most of us have so much stuff and so many activities which make life extremely complex. With all the things that occupy our time, we'll have days, weeks, and sometimes even years that pass by without ever having the chance to reflect on what we've done. Without taking the time to "wake up and smell the coffee", we can't appreciate the aromas of the beverage, and while the coffee may smell good, we move too fast to notice. Too much complexity leading to a hurried life can make experiences feel as if they never even happened! You've heard the saying, "Where'd the time go?" How sad it must feel for some people to look back on their time on Earth and ask, "Where'd my life go?" This must be avoided.

A few of us have too much time and not enough to do, but most of us are too complex and have too little time. Think of complexity on a scale of one to a hundred. A bird ranks at one, with doing little more than satisfying basic survival needs. Nearing the one hundred level of complexity would be someone like Donald Trump. This is a man who manages billion-dollar companies, television shows, beauty pageants, books, and is always working on multiple projects simultaneously. He says he loves his work and believes you're either working all the time or never working at all. He'll do whatever he can to compete in the world of business and has even trained his body to require less sleep to have more hours for productivity. His mind, or so I would think, is always racing. For me, his life is too complex. I think many would agree.

Looking at a bird's life, doing nothing more than eating and keeping warm is a little too simple for me; especially without being able to fly. Everyone has different levels of complexity they prefer and various levels they can manage. What's important is enjoying your own personal level and how your time was spent. If someone feels he should be doing more with his life, or feels he's too busy, it's time for a change.

All of us rank between one and one hundred on this scale of complexity. A lot of people are so busy that they can't appreciate life. Some are so afraid of failure that they make every effort to avoid trying anything. Where do you rank? Do you enjoy your level of complexity?

Imagining our lives with nothing can really help in answering these questions, so, rather than looking at your life as it is today, with bills, work, and everything else, start with a clean slate. While you certainly won't be able to literally eliminate every possession and obligation in your life, do so in your mind. You'll find it much easier adding to nothing than taking away from the many tasks which occupy your days and weeks.

One advantage to living in America is having choices; choices that some others do not. You can decide to become a doctor, where you want to attend school, and what kind of doctor you'd like to be. You can invent something, patent it, market it, sell it, and spend your earnings any way you wish. You can travel, drive around from state to state, then return to your home whenever you'd like. You can buy land and build a house, or even write and publish a book!

In America, one of the richest and freest counties in the world, we have tremendous imagination and creativity, and it's because we are given options. Imagine if you were born in a communist country and lived in a house identical to every other. If you worked the same number of hours as everyone else without the opportunity to earn more or less, you would probably have a much different mindset than you do today. Or, pretend you were born into an African tribe living in tents and forced to spend all day satisfying survival needs. If your day was comprised of finding enough food and water to keep you alive for the next 24 hours, you wouldn't have time for other choices. America is spoiled compared to many countries, giving us vast opportunities which we can choose to take advantage of, or take for granted.

Determine what choices you want to make by starting from scratch and envisioning your life with zero possessions. Not only do you have no money, car, or place to call home, but you also don't have any clothes, food, or water. So, picture yourself in your birthday suit with nothing more than the ability to hear, taste, touch, smell, and see.

Picture yourself lying naked outside under a public bridge with a temperature of 50 degrees Fahrenheit. That's chilly, especially with no clothes. Your first goal would probably be to find some form of clothing so you could go in public without being arrested. Then again, even being in prison could be viewed as an improvement to your current situation. At least in a jail cell you have food, water, and clothing. Valuing freedom, you don't want to go to jail, so after finding some clothes, you would need food and water. Luckily, with a mild climate, you don't need to worry about keeping warm or avoiding a heat stroke. You'll survive outside, so while it certainly isn't living in luxury, sleeping under a public bridge would not kill you.

After satisfying some basic survival needs, what would you work for, seek out and find worth pursuing? I value sleep and would want a bed. Even with this one basic desire, an array of choices is presented. In order to ensure my effort for a bed does not go in vain, I need to look at what I'm ultimately trying to accomplish. My real goal is not to earn money to buy a bed, but to obtain something to sleep on that's relatively more comfortable than the ground. Would I need a conventional 50 lb. mattress with springs and padding, or could I get an air mattress? If I did want a conventional mattress, would I need an apartment, condo or house to keep it, or could it be in a vehicle of some kind? With the air mattress, could I inflate it at night and then carry it around deflated during the day, or would I need a place to store it? Is buying a mattress my only option to improve my quality of sleep, or could I perhaps make something using readily available materials I could find? I could type a hundred pages and only skim the surface of that one relative need; bedding.

Picture yourself homeless under a bridge with nothing but ample time to your name. What would you do? Visualize your life precisely how you would want it to look without any restrictions and begin viewing every aspect of life questioning what could be. If you drink coffee in the morning, ask yourself why you drink coffee and think of other options. You could be drinking tea, a different brand of coffee, or drinking nothing at all. You could brew the coffee different ways or drink it in different places. Could you be drinking coffee in a different city or on another continent? What do you like about the coffee? Do you like the taste and smell, or just the caffeine? Is there a better way to ingest caffeine? If caffeine's for energy, is there a better way to feel energized? Start asking why while looking at other options. By getting in this habit, a world of endless possibilities and opportunities will begin to appear.

I'll be the first to confess that I'm nowhere near perfect at this. Just last year my wife and I moved into a condo with a nice living room and I immediately began thinking of how to furnish it. We ended up furnishing the room properly: With a couch, coffee table, stand for a 42" flat screen TV, DVD rack on the side of the stand, and a couple of plants at both ends of the room. A framed canvas print centered over the couch, a floor lamp held pictures and candles, a smaller lamp in the corner of the room balanced the light, and a wall clock was visible from every angle. Our living room looked great.

From Mainland to Maui

About a month later, I felt disappointed by our limited mindset while furnishing the room. I enjoyed our living room, but when looking at the choices we'd made, I saw how many options we had not considered. We made many choices; what size TV to buy, where to put the couch, and what color of TV stand to get; just to name a few, but we never asked whether we even wanted a couch at all. The couch was implied, for every living room has a couch. We never questioned whether to get a TV, because that's just what you do. Everybody has a TV.

When I began realizing our limited thinking, I stepped back to look at the well-appointed room. I pictured the empty space and saw a room with endless possibilities. We could have filled it with plants and made it feel like a green house. We could have covered it with padding and turned it into a gym. We could have left it empty and had friends over to play in a band. We could have done anything! Instead, we bought what everyone has in their living room; couch, TV, and coffee table. How thoughtless!

This was a real eye-opener for me, and also somewhat humbling. Viewing myself as a creative thinker, I now realize how I failed in not asking myself what I wanted. Instead, I let society choose for me.

This is one example of the thousands of options I personally overlooked. Had I only used my imagination and started at zero, our living room could have been spectacular. I could have been lying in a hammock watching an aquarium full of exotic fish rather than sitting on the couch flipping through channels. I couldn't choose, because I couldn't see my options. In picturing life (or an empty space) with a clean slate, it's easy to see how options are truly unlimited.

Identifying Your Driver

If you want to eat, it's (usually) because you're hungry. If you feel the urge to go to the bathroom, it's because your body's digestive system is working properly. If you want something, it's because you have a driver presenting that desire. Instead of thoughtlessly doing things because they either "need" done or because you've done them in the past, stop to ask why. What's the goal and motivating factor? What are you trying to accomplish?

To identify your driver (what you find to be worth your efforts and irreplaceable time), look at what you've done in the past. What have you done that made you feel anxious beforehand, an adrenaline rush during, and a tremendous feeling of accomplishment afterward? Was it traveling abroad, driving, bowling, cooking, rock climbing, or spending time with your family? Perhaps it was getting a promotion at work or receiving an award. Maybe it was having a child or acing a test. What have you done that's made you proud? Recall the time you were living rather than just surviving. You may be struggling to think of anything you've done that has given you joy and lasting excitement. If this is the case, think of another person you admire. Could you mimic what's made them so admirable?

For everything we do there's a driver encouraging that action to be taken. I believe the reason many of us are not fully satisfied with life is because we do things we don't necessarily want to do yet do them anyway because other people have convinced us we should. Money is a goal many people share, but what is behind that goal? We've all fantasized about what we would do with a million dollars, but I'd rather look at my goals and preferences leaving money out of the equation. In taking this approach, it's unlikely one million dollars would be required to make that dream come true. So, instead of dreaming about being a millionaire, picture your ideal life and then determine what it will take for this dream to become reality. In order to have true lasting success, we need to know what we want.

Know What You Want

If you're outside and it's cold, what would you want? You may answer by saying you want a hat, coat, or gloves. If I were to then ask you why, you would say it was because you are cold. But going further, you would want more clothes because being cold isn't physically comfortable, and to be warmer would give your body more comfort. The nerves in your skin would be telling your brain this preference. In this example, you would want to be warmer, and that would be the goal, and the means to this goal would be more clothes. This would be either a survival need or relative need, depending on the temperature and health of the individual. This is a very basic example, but how do you know what you want when pertaining to legacy needs?

Identifying the driver for your legacy needs is hard, and it's easy to become convinced that finding and pursuing it is simply too difficult. One thing that makes it such a challenge is society. Society belittles the importance of legacy needs and dwells on relative needs to the point where we are left with no time to go further. In the world in which we live, dreams and what we love the most aren't defined as needs at all. Instead, we are bombarded with the belief that our passions are just what we want and nothing more.

If our legacy needs are suppressed, our time can be wasted on things we've been convinced are necessary or worthy of our time. Our dreams become wishes; impossible fairytales rather than plans and achievable goals. In today's world, if someone is doing what they really want, it's labeled a hobby that's done in their "free time". Can you see why we're so unhappy? Believing that life is unfair becomes our reality under the misconception that our dreams are nothing more than hopes, and like Benjamin Franklin once said, "He that lives upon hope will die fasting." When legacy needs are not met or pursued, life becomes a job, where every day becomes a never-ending task to survive comfortably while not breaking the law by performing various chores we'd rather not be doing. Is this the American dream?

So, what is required and how can we get more time? Looking at our four needs, you could compromise your body and stop eating and drinking, but even though it would save time, it wouldn't end in a lively fashion. You could compromise your integrity needs, although I'm not sure how much time would be saved when doing what's right is most often avoiding what's wrong. Then there are relative needs...

There are some luxuries in life we value and others we don't. Ironically, some of those we don't really care about, we work for anyway. I feel that because we spend approximately one third of our lives asleep, a comfortable bed is well worth the time and effort it takes to acquire and maintain. I also think a cell phone is a wonderful piece of technology which adds tremendous convenience. Having the capability to call any person, place or business anytime from anywhere is fantastic, but I have no desire to take pictures, browse the internet, play video games, listen to music or do anything else on my cell phone other than making and receiving calls. Appearing relatively archaic, I have what most would consider a "basic" cell phone. It does have a built-in calculator, which I never use, but that's about it. Many folks have all the bells and whistles on their cell phones without even considering whether they're worth the time and effort it takes to pay for them. They haven't decided what they wanted but have chosen how to spend a portion of their time and effort based on what others have.

From Mainland to Maui

Look at your material possessions and determine what you enjoy and what's worth your time and effort to acquire, store, clean, and maintain. Don't buy into the game of relative needs if you don't want to. I'm not necessarily saying that pursuing nicer things is a terrible way to spend your time, but, if we want to have peace about what we're doing with our life, we must make sure it's a conscious decision. It's easier in theory than putting into practice, but start asking yourself questions about what you're doing, why you're doing it, and if the rewards are worth the effort.

Let's say you have a relatively large house. Why? Do you really enjoy the house, or does its upkeep take away from time you'd rather spend doing other things? Why sharpen a pencil if you won't use it to write? Why change the oil of a car if it sits in the garage? Why own a house with nine rooms when you only spend time in three of them?

If you discover there are things in your life you don't truly value, consider getting rid of these items, but be forewarned, letting go of what we've worked hard for is a frightening thought. I know as I've been there; twice. It's nerve-wracking to part with things you've acquired, have memories with, and enjoy knowing you have. We all like our stuff, and to picture life without it can be unimaginable, despite the potential of gaining more time for more enjoyable things.

Picturing life with fewer possessions, lower societal standings, or altered lifestyles is difficult. Through years of acquiring, you've unknowingly played the relative needs game and have moved up on the leader board. To quit now puts you at risk of being viewed as a failure in the eyes of your competition. By quitting or forfeiting various relative needs, you'll have accomplished your goal of getting more time, but also been stripped of your status as a player in these popular competitions. Sliding down the ladder you've worked hard to ascend can be more challenging than climbing up it in the first place; especially if it's the only thing you've worked to accomplish.

You may be thinking, "Who cares if I live in a smaller house so I can have more time to do other things? Who cares if I have a cheaper car, wear used clothes or take fewer vacations? I'm in charge of my own life and nobody's going to impact me or try to tell me what to do. Who cares what I do?" This is a good question. The sad and frightening reality is...EVERYONE! Everybody cares what you do, and they express it every day. While hard to believe, they've done it your entire life. Other people have influenced, persuaded, and limited you, and they've done so without your recognition.

Look At Your "Self"

In trying to determine what you truly value, view yourself from an outsider's perspective. This can be used to view the present, past, future, a specific situation, job, action, relationship, or virtually anything. Start by viewing yourself in this very moment. See what you're wearing, the piece of furniture you're sitting on, and the room you're in. How do you look? Better yet, what emotion do you have when seeing yourself from this point of view? Pretend the person reading this book is not you, but someone else. Let's call that someone, "Real". Does Real look comfortable and healthy, appearing joyful and at peace? Are you proud of Real by reading this book, or do you think Real should be doing something else? How about Real's environment? Do you like the décor, lighting, and where they're sitting? If you could choose to be anywhere in the world doing anything you wanted, is this where you would be? Is Real doing exactly what you'd be doing given the unlimited possibilities?

In visualizing your self, you may not like what you see. You may feel you should be doing something else, in a different place, or looking a different way. By looking at "Real" and using honesty, you can learn more about your preferences.

Pretend you're in college listening to your economics professor lecturing about the Federal Reserve System. If you were to be looking at this person, what would you think? Would you feel proud of whom you now know as Real? Does Real look excited about the present moment? Imagining yourself as an outsider, ask yourself if you would like to walk in Real's shoes?

Perhaps you're sitting in an office cubicle typing reports. Of all the places in the world and all the things you could be doing, would this be your preference? Pretend you're at home sitting on the couch flipping through 500 channels of television trying to determine what to watch. Of life's many options, is that what you've deemed the best choice? Are there other options?

Again, viewing Real and determining what your thoughts are of that person will reveal a lot. It may spark negative emotions and can be an uncomfortable exercise to do. But it is an exercise, and exercise usually tends to be uncomfortable. However, if you are discouraged by what you see, rather than just getting sad or disappointed, let these feelings help reveal who you are and what you find worth doing.

You can do this exercise of taking an outsider's perspective with any and every aspect of your life. It's much easier looking at someone else and judging whether or not you agree with what they're doing versus looking at yourself from an internal point of view. When introspectively evaluating yourself, it's easy to subconsciously lie, protecting your ego while hindering success. Being content with mediocrity is too easy when we only view ourselves while brushing our teeth and combing our hair. Taking a third person's perspective can help tremendously in seeing reality. We can better see who is "Real" rather than who we want to see, or who our minds tell us we are.

Fear and Honesty

There will always be highs and lows in life. We will get angry, sad, and frustrated, but we can at least have peace about our decisions. If you try defending your current position by convincing yourself that you are content when you're not, success is impossible. You'll only be hurting yourself, for no one else is responsible for you. No one else cares if you deceive yourself to pretend life is good while knowing deep down you want different. While pretending you're happy can gain popularity, it also can create a false image of happiness and recipe for failure. Any effort to get better, be different, or accomplish anything will be futile without honesty.

There may be a goal you've had for a long time, and while it could be what you find worth doing, there's a possibility it's not. This false dream could be what I call an "illusory goal". Illusory goals are facades created by other people, cultures, societies, families, and outside influences. While they may seem appealing, these illusory goals are nothing more than glamorized relative needs which always lead to unhappiness. In order to avoid them, it's important to question and carefully consider whatever you choose to pursue. Chasing illusory goals is putting effort toward something not worth doing and will only end in disappointment. Avoiding these could potentially be the greatest challenge toward attaining success.

Another challenge to face when considering how we should be living and what we should be doing is fear. If fear causes you to ignore a situation because it's difficult to modify, you've already failed. Fear can appear in many ways, forms, and from all kinds of sources. Fear can also be extremely deceptive, appearing as false protection by stopping us before even getting started on a goal. To reach success and happiness, we need to confront our fears, accepting that change will not come easily and will most likely include risk. But like the saying goes, "nothing ventured, nothing gained".

The truth can be one of the most frightening things in the world when viewing how you live, how you think, and what you value; but can also be the most liberating. Confronting harsh realities is the first step toward changing for the better. As they say in self-help groups, the first step toward recovery is admitting you have a problem. Do you have a problem with your life? Could it be better? Could you be better?

Keep honesty in mind when thinking about how you got to where you are. The path you've taken may have been ugly, but tomorrows doesn't have to be. Those who ignore history are destined to repeat it, and if your life's great, keep doing whatever you're doing. But if something could change for the better, then do something different. Regardless of what your life looks like now, stop, for it's only after you stop when you're free to think about the past and what's influenced who you are today.

Stop Everything

- Stop what you're doing before taking action
- Routine can be good, but can also lead to a lack of thinking
- Everything in life has needs
    - Survival needs are food, water, and protection from the elements
    - Relative needs are life's comforts, all of which take time and effort to acquire and maintain
    - Integrity needs are simply doing what's right
    - Legacy needs are what is required to have true success, reach full potential, and go beyond one's self
- Picturing our lives with nothing can help reveal hidden options

- A driver is the reason behind the effort you're putting forth

- We can rid ourselves of certain possessions and statuses we don't truly value to free more time for legacy needs

- Satisfied legacy needs are permanent, while relative needs are always temporary

- View yourself as an outsider to help determine your preferences and feelings about your life

- Illusory goals are desires created by others

- Confronting fear and being honest with yourself and others are required for success

T. Think About Your Past

Think (v.)- to employ one's mind rationally and objectively in evaluating or dealing with a given situation

How often do you think? Without much thought you may say you think all the time. But do you honestly think consciously and objectively as defined by the dictionary? I'll be the first to admit that while I do think a lot, I'm usually not doing it consciously. Continuing to be honest, I oftentimes think with my own subjective emotions and feelings rather than rationally and objectively. To think both consciously and objectively is not something we do naturally and is usually reserved for school and work assignments; not personal life.

If you're lost in a frozen forest, you're doomed if you run around sporadically looking for a trail. You first have to stop. But if you stop and do nothing more, you'll freeze to death. After you stop you must think, but instead of immediately thinking of solutions to unpleasant situations, first think of how you got to where you are today. How did you get lost? Are you really lost? How did you physically get to your current location? If you are lost, do you care enough to try to get back on the trail?

In order to plan for tomorrow, evaluate where you were yesterday. This is a task more easily spoken than performed since most of us have been driving so fast to get to the finish line (retirement, vacation, home ownership, weekend, etc.) we've ignored the road we've taken. We haven't given any attention to the journey but have solely focused on the reward at the end. It's for this reason that remembering how we got to where we are today can be quite difficult. However, retracing our steps is a vitally important action toward accomplishing anything outside the realm of our daily routine.

Past Time

The past is a funny thing. It influences what we enjoy and dislike, it molds how we view the world, and can even define who we are. If someone is notorious for something they've done in the past, it creates a reputation that affects how they're viewed by others. Is this a bad thing? It isn't good or bad; it's a fact. This being the case, how can we use our past for creating a more positive and fulfilling future? Think about it but do so as objectively and unbiased as possible. Again, this can be done by trying to view your past from an outsider's perspective.

Envisioning the way a previous event truly took place is impossible, while viewing it as perceived is inevitable. What I mean is that every person has a different perception, and this perception is largely influenced by the individual's past experiences, in addition to their hopes for the future.

For example, if a person has driven the same route to work for many years without an accident, there would be no reason for them on any particular day to expect one, or even give the idea a thought. Compare that to a person who is getting in the car for the first time following an injury accident. These two people could be driving the same road, on the same day, at the same time, yet have very different experiences based on their individual perceptions. The person who had recently been in an accident could be driving more cautiously and with fear, while the accident-free driver could be without concern and enjoying his time. If you've ever received a speeding ticket, the following day, and for many days after, you may drive slower and keep watch for police. The only difference with the present is due to something that has happened in the past.

Hope for the future can also influence our perception. This is different than plans for the future. Future plans pertain more to actions, while future hopes relate to mindset. Someone could be in an abusive relationship and get beaten every day. To an outsider, the pain could appear as unbearable, yet to the person being abused who is hoping for a greater future, this could seem tolerable.

How do you perceive your own past and how is that perception affecting your present? Throughout our lives we've learned many things. Through our parents, co-workers, friends, media, teachers, and superiors, we've gained perspectives on how we view individual things and life as a whole. If you had identical twins sitting side by side who had been separated at birth, raised by different people in different social classes, and attended different schools in different cities, they would be very different. If you were to then ask these two people a series of questions pertaining to their opinions on various things, you would most likely receive different answers.

Without trying to label or judge your past, think about everything that has occurred since birth. Whether this past gives you positive or negative emotions, think about how you can use it to your benefit. What have you learned through the struggles you've encountered? What knowledge have you gained through work experiences, and what have you done that you've enjoyed? What do you want more of, less of, and what have you done in the past that has made you proud? Think about these things and write them down to mold your life to what you envision to be ideal.

In the following section I've outlined a life that could easily be yours. While everyone obviously has had different childhood experiences and various things which have influenced them, I've written it to demonstrate a point - we have been born into a world of rules. We live in a society of routines and common practices, many of which are never given thought. We do things based on tradition, and rarely question the origin or practicality of what's viewed as the norm. So, in reading the following section, think about the influences you personally have had since you were born. Bring to focus the rules you've been given to decide whether or not you want to follow them. While many rules are set to protect liberties, other rules can restrict potential.

Growing Up

The following section goes through the life of a fictional character. This could be you...

You were born in a hospital. Immediately upon birth, you were cleaned, named, given a Social Security Number and a bracelet for identification. You were vaccinated, fingerprinted, and possibly, if you were like me, placed into a small box (incubator) for monitoring. Maybe you were born healthy or maybe you had some complications. Either way, you survived birth and are smothered by the affection of random strangers (your family and friends of the family) wanting to hold you. In the next several days you'll be heading home with your mother to mark the start of your new life.

After getting home, your mom introduces you to your nursery; blues or pinks, depending on your gender, with shapes of unknown objects all over. You won't be spending much time here until you get a little older but will be sleeping in a crib in your parents' room.

Before long, you graduate from your parents' bedroom to your nursery. You are then upgraded to a larger crib with bars that you can grip onto and look out from. You enjoy your new crib and have plenty of space to move around. In your closet are lots of clothes piled on the floor and flooding the hangers. With so many new clothes, every day you wear a new outfit. Your mother knows you have too many yet refuses to return them or give them away. Most of the clothes were gifts, and she doesn't feel right getting rid of them.

Several months later you are one year old. Happy birthday! Your family celebrates with cameras, presents, tons of food, and a cake. A cake? Why should a one-year old baby have cake? But of course, it's a birthday party, and what birthday party would be complete without birthday cake?! Your dad opens your presents while pondering where they'll be stored and proceeds to thank everyone on your behalf. You smile in your high chair, spit out your candle, smear cake on your face, and look forward to never remembering your first birthday.

As the years pass and you get a little older, you receive more toys and gifts. With all this new stuff, your house is beginning to resemble an oversized storage unit, so your parents decide to buy a bigger house. Upon moving into your new house, your parents introduce you to your room; with a bed! The room isn't big, but huge in comparison to your crib. Although very different, this room is like your crib in many ways. It's shaped the same (square or rectangle), and instead of having the bars to look out from, it has windows! This is your new box, with ample room to crawl around in and play; your room.

You've made it to five years old! You've learned to walk and talk and are now ready for your first day of school. You feel good about the way you look, with a fresh haircut and new outfit for your first day. This is a very important day, for not only is it your first day of school but is also the first day you'll be graded. The competition is on, but you are oblivious. You're just looking forward to recess. You can't wait to get outside to run around and play as a reward for your completed schoolwork and cooperative behavior. When school's out, more time to play! Life is good.

You love learning in school, but as the years go by you begin learning more than just reading, writing, and arithmetic; you start learning about life. You learn in school and at home that if you do what you're told you will be rewarded with free time, good food, and compliments. All of these rewards encourage you and raise your self-esteem. You learn that the better you dress and nicer you look the better you're treated. You begin noticing how the teachers and classmates act toward the other students based on how they look, talk, and think. You learn that the better you play sports the more you're liked by your coaches and peers. Your teachers give you special privileges because you get straight A's, and your parents reward you for following the rules. You get praised and treated well for keeping the status quo and being a fun, easy-going child. So, you strive to be better at sports, better at schoolwork, more obedient, and better dressed in order to be treated nicer and receive better rewards.

After enjoying your childhood, you are now thirteen. Things are changing and getting more complicated now. Your body is feeling and looking strange, and some of your classmates are even belittling you for no apparent reason. Your classmates of the opposite sex are also appearing and acting much different than in years past. What's going on?!

You come to your parents in bewilderment, asking for an explanation of all the changes. They explain puberty, give the sex talk, and continue to explain that it's human nature to compete. It's the competitive drive that makes some people jealous and act mean, but that it's not a bad thing as it helps us grow as human beings. It's what drives us to be better, helps regulate cost, and provides more conveniences, nicer luxuries, and greater innovation. They even quote Herbert Hoover, "Competition is not only the basis of protection to the consumer but is the incentive to progress." America is one of the lucky places to have competition so anyone can become wealthy and have more through hard work. Unfortunately, some people are envious of those who are smarter, have more, or have a more attractive appearance, and sometimes get upset because they are jealous. Your parents continue their lecture, explaining that envious people will try to bring you down, so they'll feel better about themselves.

You apply the concepts you were taught by your parents throughout middle and high school by working hard to get good grades. You keep good hygiene and do what you're told. With a few exceptions, you're well liked, treated well, and rewarded for your efforts.

Upon nearing your junior year in high school, you start paying more attention to the A's, B's, and C's on your report cards and start thinking about college. Upon meeting with your guidance counselor, she adores you, and says you are a model student.

You continue excelling through college and into the workforce, pleasing your bosses and gaining promotions; being successful. After working for thirty years, you have a decent amount of money in the bank and choose to retire. Another conventional party is thrown with more cake; another ritualistic celebration for customary dates and events with traditional decorations and ceremonial events of unknown meaning and origin. Once retired, you golf, watch television, sleep, and do anything you wish with no obligations or need to produce an income. You don't have to work, so you don't.

A year later you become bored and realize your pension, along with the money you've saved over the years, really isn't that much. Retirement, it seems, appeared more appealing from the working side of the fence. Is this what life was all about? Was all the hard work chasing "The American Dream" really worth it?

You begin reflecting on your life and what could have been; but what really could have been? What could you have done differently? You did what you were told and worked hard, were rewarded with vacations, houses, cars, and clothes, and are now retired. But was it all worth it?

That Was life???

Many of us have played the game of Monopoly and know the goal is to buy property, build houses, and eventually take out the competition through their possessions. It's a game with many similarities to the capitalistic system we have in the United States. But what happens at the end of the game? Someone is declared the winner, and then everything is stripped from the board and put back in the box. Monopoly is like our life in that in the end everything goes away.

Was what I did yesterday, last week, last year, or in the last thirty years really the best way I could have spent my time and energy? Sadly, many of us have never had the time to ask these questions. With school, parties, sports, vacations, cell phones, computers, portfolios, video games, TV, church, exercise, shopping, traffic jams, children, holidays, relationships, musical instruments, doctors' appointments, stereo systems, movies, pets, oil changes, gardening, dishes, vacuuming, sleeping, eating, drinking, and having sex, there was simply no time. As a kid you had school, homework, extracurricular activities, and friends, and after all that was done, you usually just wanted to watch TV or play a computer game. You may have had a part-time job through high school. In college, you had relationships, a 3.0 GPA, bartending shifts a few nights a week, and were lucky to get six hours of sleep. There was certainly no time in the workforce for self-evaluation, for that time was spent competing for more money, a better position, "job security" and "financial independence". Through the e-mails and phone calls, long commutes, continuing education and corporate meetings, there was barely an hour to spend with your family.

In every year of your life you've been deprived of a 31, 7, or even 2 day period to really stop and think. You've used your mind in school and work, but have never thought about yourself, by yourself, for yourself; for your heart. You never looked at "Real" to see if he was pursuing his most fulfilling desires. You chose to go to college, but never decided what you truly wanted to accomplish. You worked hard to retire, but never thought about what you wanted to do in retirement, and you pursued promotions at work before considering how those pay raises could be spent. You've never taken time to view yourself from across the room and recognize the importance of understanding who you are. You never stripped off your clothes which displayed advertisements for Polo and Nike and stood naked in front of the mirror knowing that what you see is all you have. Your mind, body, and spirit are all you truly have. Your vision has been distorted by status, clothing, money, and possessions, and you haven't decided to be precisely the person you are by ignoring society's promoted facades. You never dreamed of doing what you love the most, the majority, or all of your time. You've never had the chance to look past the status quo, feel gravity hold you down and perceive everything as temporary and tangible. No one ever said, "Hey! Take a minute to think about how life's working for you." Is life working for you, or are you just working for life?

Think About Your Past

- To think means to consciously and objectively employ your mind
- Our past influences our present
- Growing up we had many routines scheduled by others
- Are you spending your time in the best way possible?
- How's life working for you?

O. Observe Your Environment

Observe (v.)- To see, watch, perceive, or notice

After thinking about your past and how you've arrived at where you are today, take some time to observe your environment; environment defined as the totality of surrounding conditions.

There are two things which comprise environment. The biggest difference between the two is that we have the potential to control the first entirely; our mind. While it's possible to moderately manipulate physical environments, external situations outside of our mental state are not in our control. Some would argue that our minds are not part of our environment, but when looking at the definition, "totality of surrounding conditions", do our minds not affect how we feel, what we think, and the condition of every second?

There are many elements of our environment, but only one that we can have complete control over. To take advantage of this, we need to understand the difference between our self and our mind. Our mind is a wonderful and fascinating tool, but only when used properly by understanding that it is just one part of our body.

Sensual Exercise

Before looking at your mind and how it affects your environment, take note of your physical surroundings. While it would be easy for me to say to take five minutes to close your eyes and picture your life, the task is too daunting. There is simply too much happening every minute, much of which we don't even notice. This "Sensual Exercise" can help form thoughts about your individual preferences. These preferences can lead to success by always doing what we know to be worth our resources.

Our brain is one of the most fascinating and complex things in the world. Sadly, with so much complexity in our modern age, it's nearly impossible to give thought to everything we're experiencing. Everything our body is transmitting to our brain moves so fast and is gone in the blink of an eye, making it hard to comprehend what's taking place in the moment. There's too much information that comes all at once, all the time.

The more we learn about our brain the more questions we have. One thing we do know is that most people are given five senses; hearing, smelling, seeing, feeling, and tasting. All day our brain transmits these senses. This can be overwhelming, as only one organ, the brain, is trying to tell us what all of our other body parts are simultaneously saying.

How do you feel this hour, this minute, and this second? We rarely give this question much thought, so in an effort to fully experience and comprehend what we're doing, focus on only one sense at a time. You can do this nearly any time of the day with obvious exceptions. I don't recommend closing your eyes to concentrate on what you're hearing while driving a car, but you get the idea.

Try it now. First, what do you smell? Close your eyes and plug your ears if you prefer. Is the smell pleasant? Can you smell anything at all?

How about touch? How is your body feeling right now? How's the temperature? Do your clothes feel comfortable against your body? Do you have any pain or discomfort on your skin or in your muscles? Can you feel your heart beating? Can you feel your lungs expanding and contracting with each breath?

Move onto taste. You're probably not eating anything right now, but how does your mouth taste? Does it taste clean and fresh, or stale and hot? Can you taste anything?

What do you hear? Have you ever heard silence? Is what you hear comforting, or is it unpleasant and causing you anxiety?

Lastly, give attention to your sight. We frequently take this sense for granted but put your other senses to rest for a moment and really see. Let your eyes tell your mind what you see, instead of the other way around. What do you see? Is it vivid and bright, or dull and gray? Do you like what you see?

A great challenge to this exercise is allowing your senses to tell you what you're experiencing and using your mind as a transmitter to your true self. Unfortunately, we oftentimes do the opposite by allowing our mind to tell us what it's experiencing, and our mind can be deceiving. To better process information, our minds will label, categorize, and compare things relative to what we've seen in the past. Understanding the way in which past influences can mold how we perceive life explains why something may look one way to you, yet different to someone else. Keeping this in mind, work on perceiving what is, rather than what you pre-determine or assume it to be.

What Is Real?

In the movie *The Matrix*, Morpheus asks Neo, "What is real?" He continues with saying, "If real is simply what you can feel, taste, smell, and see, then real is simply electrical signals interpreted by your brain."

The reality is that we are human beings with more than just a brain and have needs which far exceed our mind's boundaries.

We want to invent, create, advance, be pushed, and compete, but our mind wants a candy bar. The electrical signals interpreted by our brains want us to feel good, taste sweet foods, and smell fresh roses. They want sugar, spice, and everything nice, and until we can overpower our minds from years of programming, we will continue putting immediate sensual gratification before our greatest desires, keeping our legacy needs a second priority. Being aware that our minds want to feel good every moment can be invaluable in giving your legacy driver more urgency and importance.

The brain is a tool that wants to benefit and protect. It wants to be comfortable, which can conflict with our dreams when working to shield us from discomfort. If I see a red-hot stovetop burner, I won't touch it because my mind says it would hurt. Touching a hot stove will only give blistered fingers, but what if by touching the stove I gained greatness? Would it be worth it?

Let's say your goal is to lose twenty pounds. You know it would be amazing to look and feel better, and you have taken all the necessary steps toward making that dream a reality. You've designed a plan to cater specifically to you, your desires, strengths, and weaknesses, and can clearly envision yourself making it happen. It's a presumptive belief that these unwanted pounds were most likely gained by pleasing your senses with great tasting food. Therefore, your heart's desire to lose weight must overpower your mind's desire to eat junk food. But, if your heart is not strong enough, the mind will win, and the goal will be lost.

In this example, your mind says a cheeseburger will make you happy and that lying on the couch watching television is what you truly want. This calling is not yourself and will not fulfill your dream of losing weight. This isn't a negative thing, it's just your mind doing its job in wanting to feel good and please the senses. Are our minds supposed to hinder us? Absolutely not! If you touch a hot stove, your mind tells you it's hurting your body. If you're rock climbing and look down hundreds of feet to what would be your death if you let go, your mind tells you to (literally) hang on for dear life. It tells us these things because it's learned that a red stovetop is painful to touch, and that gravity will pull you to the Earth and kill you. The mind doesn't want us to feel pain and has learned many "not to do's", but it's also learned many "good to dos. It's learned that candy tastes good, roses smell sweet, music sounds nice, and sunsets over the ocean are pleasing to eye.

While pleasing our senses is inarguably enjoyable, to constantly stimulate the mind in an attempt to be ultimately happy is futile. It's useless because by feeding one desire we disappoint another. We live in a world that contradicts itself, with advertisements of healthy people eating fast food and models with bright white teeth smoking cigarettes. We've been taught that a college degree is required to get a good job and be successful without first evaluating success or what constitutes a good way to produce an income. We've been told the world is a dangerous place, so we sit in our living rooms engulfed in screens while daydreaming of traveling to exotic destinations. We've grown up believing the more stuff we have the better off we are, only to be frustrated with the lack of time these things leave us with. We go to work and look forward to the weekend, then dread going back on Monday. At home, in the car, at work, and in school, we compare ourselves to others and enviously want more. But what do we really want?

Discover What You Want

You may despise something about yourself while admiring something else. You may absolutely hate your job but love your sense of humor; detest where you live but cherish your car. While I know its cliché, writing down these observations can teach you who you are and what you truly value. You can find what you wish to change, alter, or abolish, and how strong those desires are.

When writing down your life's pros and cons, get as specific as possible. During the "Sensual Exercise", you may find that your bedroom stinks, the lighting in your bathroom irritates you, or you prefer the feel of carpet on your feet rather than hard tile. These examples are all very basic, but they are a start. If you can't determine whether you prefer ketchup over mustard, making a life changing decision will be impossible. After recognizing your preferences on small things, you can then begin to move on to bigger choices, eliminating what you don't like and expanding on what you do.

Consider how the things you value can be better and how you can have more time for your life's passions. Let's pretend you enjoy gardening more than anything else. With a limited mindset, you may think of spending more time or money on nicer plants or newer tools. These are basic and obvious options, but by expanding your thinking you can find countless ideas for possible improvements. First, what's your driver? In other words, what do you like about gardening? Can you garden all year round where you currently live? Do you prefer nurturing flowers or growing vegetables? What vegetables do you prefer? Could you sell your flowers or vegetables? Could gardening produce an income in other ways? Could you own a greenhouse and garden all year-round? Perhaps you could be the first home gardener who plants flowers on the moon. Who knows? The point is that anything can be improved and nearly everything can be removed. Asking questions will expand your imagination to give you ideas, and these ideas can become choices and goals which make for a more fulfilled life.

When looking at what we dislike or don't truly value, we need to see if these things could be altered or completely eliminated. Looking at another basic example, let's say you hate cutting the grass. Could you pay someone to cut the grass? Could you get fake grass? Could you move to a city, house, or apartment that doesn't have grass to cut? Is cutting your grass even necessary?

Life's greatest and most rewarding challenge is to always be doing what you want in the best way possible all of the time. Despite how crazy it sounds, it's not impossible. Life will never be perfect, but we can at least be aware of what decisions we have and then celebrate the choices we've made.

Are You Subconsciously Defeated?

If you could eliminate anything from your life without any repercussions, without losing any luxuries or comforts, and without disappointing anyone, what would it be? Your job may be the most likely answer, and if it is, ask yourself why. Think about the rewards you gain from your job. Are these rewards the only reason you're doing it? If so, are the rewards worth it? If you've been working for six months straight and are mentally surviving on nothing other than a week's vacation at the end of the 180 day stretch, you're not living. Instead, you're spending the majority of your life enslaved to the future. If you're studying and all you can think about is snowboarding, why are you in a library? When escaping from work or school is your only motivation for working or studying, something's got to give. I'll say that again. If you are not enjoying what you are doing in a large portion of your life and are merely anticipating its completion, you need change.

Life is simply too short, and unlike a video game, our lives can't be "continued" by pushing a button.

I truly enjoy learning and value education as one of the most important things on Earth. I was never a trouble maker in high school, but I did question a lot of what most students thoughtlessly accepted. I would occasionally raise my hand to ask, "Why do we need to know this?", or, "When in life are we going to use this?" Most of the time I was ignored, but sometimes the teacher would abruptly answer, "because."

There was one time I received a sincere answer from my high school math teacher when I questioned the value of the equation we were being taught. I asked when the equation would be used in life and he responded with, "Chances are you will never use this equation in life after school unless you become a scientist or math teacher," he was brutally honest. "Truthfully, the majority of what you learn in high school will not benefit you and will be useless after you graduate. The reason you need a four-year high school diploma is to show employers you're disciplined. College is the same way. A college degree shows you can follow directions, maintain schedules, and do what you're told whether you agree or not. Essentially, you need to study in school to learn to do things you don't want to do." That was the last time I asked that question.

I appreciated his honesty, despite the sad reality of the answer I already knew to be true. If you're not going to school to become a doctor, practice law, learn how to repair cars, or study outer-space for a living, much of what is learned in school is never used. The majority of time spent doing homework, studying, and writing papers is conditioning. From K-12 and continuing through college, we are programmed to accept doing things we don't want to do. If you enjoy learning in a classroom setting at a school or university, keep it up. There is nothing wrong with competing in school so long as you enjoy the competition and have a clear understanding as to why you are doing so. I was not one of those students. I unfortunately regret the days I spent looking at the clock waiting for the final bell. In wanting the clock to move faster, I was simultaneously wishing my life would end faster. Most things in life can be retrieved, remade, repurchased, or fixed, but months, weeks, days, and minutes are not in this category.

Our society has sold us many untruths. One of the biggest and most widely accepted is that a job is mandatory. While the ability to keep your body alive does require some effort, working in a paid position is not required. This is a common misconception by most American people, despite seeing it every day. Walk down the street of any city and I guarantee you'll find at least a few people sleeping on the sidewalk who realize that having a job is an option rather than an obligation.

Am I saying the key to success is becoming homeless, eating out of a trash can and using old newspapers for blankets? Of course not! I'm simply stating the fact that to work or not to work is an option; and the option is yours. If you don't mind begging for change, being more susceptible to illness and being viewed as a lazy bum, then quit your job and become homeless. Just because your high school guidance counselor didn't discuss graduating to then live on the street doesn't change the fact that it's an option.

If in America we're all given options and can choose our own fate, why do so many of us complain without trying to change? One reason is because complaining is so commonly accepted. Complaining has not only become tolerable, but almost expected and assumed as normal! Just ask ten friends, family members or strangers about their workday. I've done it, and it's a big contributor as to why I'm writing this book! Some people are miserable and love broadcasting their misfortunes. I suppose it can be comforting getting together with people to complain about work, talk about whom in the family died, who's in the hospital, or whose kids are getting into trouble.

We commonly complain without even recognizing it while subconsciously promoting a victimized mentality. It's customary to thoughtlessly say, "Aww, I'd love to join, but I can't because I have to work." The sentence itself is not destructive or meaningfully negative, but it does carry a negative connotation which can influence the way we think and feel. People use this exact sentence without understanding what it subconsciously says to our minds; and if you say and hear it enough, you could start believing it. If you believe what you've just said, you have given yourself the mentality that life is filled with mandatory obligations. This defeated mentality can make life feel like one long endless chore.

Very few people believe skipping work would warrant an execution; possible job termination, but not a public beheading. What we mean when saying, "I can't" or, "I have to" is, "While I truly would enjoy doing something (whatever it may be), I am scheduled to work. Because I value my house, my car, hot meals, and the occasional vacation, I am going to choose my job instead. I understand the things I value cost money and that working is how I get paid. So, while I could join you for whatever fun activity you've invited me to, tomorrow I am going to work. I'd rather not risk losing my job seeing that it does provide certain comforts which I value and enjoy."

Another term we use without much thought, also subconsciously contributing to this enslaved way of thinking, is "free time". What is "free time"? "Free time" has been defined as time we don't need to work, study, or do chores. Again, while there's no harm intended by using this phrase, to separate "free time" from time we do business implies that our "business time" is somehow not free. In school we wait until 3 P.M., at work we wait until 5 P.M., and in our commutes we wait in traffic. Standing in line at the bank we wait to make our deposit. We wait to go on vacation, wait until we get paid and wait and wait and wait. With a subconsciously defeated mind that's always waiting for something, our lives appear filled with mandatory tasks just waiting to be finished. We spend life waiting to find time that's free, when truly all of our time is free and dictated by no one but us.

The last example of a dangerous phrase is "running errands". What is an errand? The dictionary defines an errand as, "a short trip that is taken in performance of a necessary task or mission". It may be necessary for something, but why do we run errands rather than walk, complete, perform, achieve, pursue, or enjoy them? What's the difference between casually shopping for a new stereo system and buying milk at the grocery store? One is fun and one is an errand. One is a privilege while one is viewed as necessary. Running errands takes the presence and fun away from the task and focuses entirely on the finish.

These are a few examples of how we subconsciously live our lives in defeat, strictly concentrated on the completion rather than the process. It's the mentality that life is not fair, and that we are required to do things we'd rather not.

What Is Success?

Everyone wants to be successful. This quest for greatness is shared throughout the world in various countries and cultures yet defined in different ways. How these groups define success has a lot to do with their starting point. How do you define success in comparison to your parents and colleagues? Were you all raised in a similar fashion?

Let's pretend you were born into an Amazonian tribe whose basic survival needs occupied all of their time. In this situation, success could be viewed as picking berries or killing an animal for food. A woman giving birth to a healthy baby could be a tremendous success. Perhaps surviving the common cold or returning from a hunting expedition in the wilderness would be successful.

How about if you were born in America to a poverty-stricken mother who never graduated from high school? To go to college (from her perspective) could be an extraordinary success. Compare that to a family of lawyers where to graduate from Harvard at the top of your class would be successful while merely graduating would be the standard. Where you start in life and the perspectives of those grading your success can be the very thing which defines it. This definition will determine how the majority of life's time and energy is spent. In the example of the tribe, what's expected is getting enough food and water for the day. By doing this, while you may not have gone above and beyond, the expectation was met by successfully surviving another day.

Looking at a more modern example, pretend you're the son or daughter of a father who is a wealthy business owner. Your father has worked hard in life and expects nothing less from you. He wants you to go to college, get a degree, and then continue growing his already profitable company. He values these things and has considered what he's accomplished to be a great success. While you respect his business and appreciate the opportunities it's afforded you, you don't want it. In fact, you want nothing to do with it. Your passion is scuba diving, and you love it so much you want to become an instructor and show others the beauty beneath the ocean's surface you've so passionately made a part of yourself. This is a "lose, lose" situation, as following in your dad's footsteps will make him proud of you, yet disappointing yourself in the process. Not only would he view you as a success, but many others would as well. Chances are that growing up having a rich father, your friends also had wealthy parents with similar ways of grading success; mainly through financial, physical, and career statuses. You know if you were to tell your friends, people you grew up with, and other acquaintances that you would prefer to teach people how to dive rather than be a millionaire business owner, they would think you were crazy! Imagine what they would say... "The dive instructor's pay can barely feed a family while owning your dad's business would reap millions. You'd never have to worry about money in your life!" In this example you would either disappoint everybody you know and have them view you as a failure, or, you do just the opposite in doing something you don't prefer.

Let's look at a similar, yet very different situation on the opposite side of society's spectrum. Let's say you are the son or daughter of a single parent struggling to make ends meet. You have four brothers and two sisters, none of whom have attended college. Not only did they not go to college, but all six of them left high school before graduating. If you were to graduate from high school, you'd be successful in the eyes of your family. You'd be surpassing your siblings in academics by finishing high school, so in the eyes of those around you, you've achieved success!

In this situation, the expectations of others could easily hinder potential. Let's say the poor high school graduate was a genius who could have graduated from high school by the age of fourteen. The point is, despite how others may view success, what's important is your individual perspective. If the student believed that true success was in graduating from college instead of just high school, was this person successful? This is where our starting point can either help or hurt our dreams.

Upon looking at these examples, you can see where starting points and expectations greatly contribute to how we view success. But what is success? I believe success can be whatever you want it to be. If you are working on a puzzle, progress or completion could be considered successful, depending on your goal. If you want to improve your golf game, practice or reaching a predetermined score could be a success. If you have a goal of owning property, you could view buying a house or just saving money for a down payment to be a success. Success is putting time and energy toward goals you decide are worth pursuing.

Life's Puzzle

Life is an evolving puzzle which completes itself in due time; time outside of our control. Everyone's puzzle is different in many ways, with different pictures, a different number of pieces, different sized pieces, and times in which the puzzle is finished. Just like a jigsaw puzzle, our life's puzzle also has two sides; one side is blank and one side shows the picture. Many of us go through life struggling because we haven't turned over the pieces to see the picture. We spend life forcing together cardboard cutouts just hoping they'll somehow combine to make progress. We need to have vision of what we're trying to solve before putting effort into our puzzle. We cannot expect life to get better without seeing what better looks like. To do so is impossible, yet we try it all the time.

By redefining success and understanding what you want, you can begin taking steps toward turning the puzzle pieces right side up. The puzzle won't make progress itself, but clearly seeing what you're trying to accomplish gives life clarity instead being frustrated by guesswork. If you decide to take over the family business rather than recognizing and pursuing your dream of becoming a dive instructor, you have failed. While you may have pleased your father, your family, your peers and colleagues, you will have defeated the dreams of the only person it directly affects; you.

David J. Gross

Success = $$ = Comforts = ??

Society disagrees with my definition of success. You don't flip on the TV and hear, "Success is whatever you want it to be! Don't worry about making money, looking good, owning a house, or driving a nice car." Instead, we see ads on how to get rich, how to buy cars and houses with no money down, and how to effortlessly lose weight in a matter of days. Society specifically measures success using two rules of measurement; money and status.

Let's first look at money and what gives it the prestige it has today. What can money buy? Money can buy two things; comforts and time. The time equation is simple. If you figure you can survive on $50 a day and have $5,000 to your name, you can survive for 100 days without earning a penny. Obviously sitting around on $50 a day twiddling your thumbs or reading a book without producing an income is not considered successful in today's world. But what if you spent those days pursuing your dream, or better yet, what if twiddling your thumbs and reading a book was your dream? Either way, time isn't valued nearly as much as comforts.

Comforts can be called conveniences, luxuries, indulgences, or pleasures. These comforts can range from basic conveniences to wildly extravagant and luxurious experiences or material goods. I define a comfort as anything other than basic food and water; and no, steak and lobster served with a chilled bottle of Perrier is not basic food and water. This meal, in addition to houses, cars, vacations, clothing, and anything that goes beyond keeping you alive is a comfort.

Comforts are nice and do as the name implies in making life more comfortable. Sadly, this is a standard our society uses to measure success. While not to say that every comfort is obtained solely to present an image, the more comforts you have and can put on display, the more successful you appear to society. The more successful you appear, the better you're treated. Realizing this fact, people can and do create the illusion they are successful just to be treated better. They'll spend time and effort earning money just to give that impression, sometimes even spending money they don't have in pursuit of that image; and this image can become a dangerous obsession.

Society has even gone so far as to advertise these comforts as more important than ethics and morals. In the eyes of society, the honest hard-working family man isn't nearly as successful as the well paid, yet dishonest business person making four times the amount of money. The working conditions of the laborers who make designer jeans are irrelevant compared to the images those brand names hold. Success is no longer defined as being good, but by having goods.

One of the most frustrating things about the way success is defined is the emphasis placed on the finish rather than the journey. The number one definition of success in today's dictionaries is, "an event that accomplishes its intended purpose". Reading more into this definition you can see how it completely takes away from the activity. An event that accomplishes its intended purpose could be winning a basketball game, but if the event of success was merely winning the game, was playing or practicing the game unsuccessful? If you enjoyed playing the game but lost, did you fail? If winning the game was the only successful part, then success is quite overrated and short-lived. If winning was the only event that was successful, how long will the winning team have success? Until they change out of their uniform? Until they physically leave the court? Until the after-party concludes, or will this feeling of success last until they lose a game? In order to have joy in our lives, we need to redefine what society has considered success.

Job titles have become a huge way of measuring prosperity in today's world. Why is a doctor or lawyer deemed more accomplished than a gardener or trash collector? Why do we consider the CEO of a profitable company a success while a painter doing what he loves is viewed as less? Job title is something that influences many decisions for a lot of people when they perceive one job as better than the next based on this alone. We've been convinced our job is who we are, and whatever career we choose is what defines us. Is this accurate?

We are individuals who want to be heroes. We want to leave a legacy and be remembered for the many great things we did in life. Some people want to be business owners and professionals in order to make lots of money so they and their families can enjoy life's comforts; and that's great! That's what makes us individuals and keeps America rising as a nation of innovators. Some people, however, do not want money and do not care about job titles or societal statuses. Some people want to surf, ski, paint, travel, and read. Some value time more than money, and as long as both groups do not compromise integrity needs, neither one is better than the other.

Are you a person who doesn't care about owning a nice car so you may one day have the opportunity to climb Mt. Everest? If you do want money and the luxuries it provides, you're not inferior to Van Gogh or less of a person than an aspiring photographer; just different. All the goals we set in life should be viewed as successful so long as they're deemed worthy of the time and effort by the individual rather than society.

Understanding "Illusory Goals"

It's understood from an early age that if you do what you're told, you will be treated well, rewarded, and applauded for your efforts. If you don't, you're treated poorly and punished in one way or another. This rule was taught at home by our parents and continued in school by our teachers. It's been made clear by our bosses, enforced through government, and has applied in all areas of life.

As a kid, if you do what you're told by your parents you receive ice cream or extra play time. If you disobey, you could be grounded or lose privileges. Talk excessively in class when you're not supposed to and you'll get detention. If you don't do your homework, you'll get a bad grade on your report card. Run a red light, speed going down the highway, or jaywalk in the street, you'll be slapped with a fine.

Many rules are great; teaching students, keeping our streets safe, and protecting lives. But certain rules can be harmful. We follow rules every day, and while many are beneficial and understood, a good portion is followed without thought.

Rules are everywhere and posted in every situation, either by visible or hidden signs. Some of these rules we know because our parents, teachers, or other mentors taught us growing up. Other rules are written down, voted on, and enforced as law. But many rules in our daily lives are unwritten, unnoticed, and oftentimes followed without benefiting or protecting us. These unperceived rules have been learned through our experiences, taught by our society, and encouraged by our families. Have you ever thought about the rules you unknowingly follow? What rules do we need to follow and why? Have they affected the way we think and the actions we take? Have they influenced our dreams and what we find of value?

The older we get, the more rules we discover. Think back to when you were five years old. You may have wanted to become a doctor, a magician, or a firefighter, but at some point, that changed. At some point growing up you learned the rules of money, and a job's primary purpose is to produce income.

David J. Gross

Some people work because they love what they do. Others enjoy their job because it provides them opportunities, satisfies survival needs, and rewards them with comforts they appreciate. But for many Americans today, money has become the only motivating factor for working and has influenced how we feel about our jobs. Many people work to pay the bills without questioning whether they appreciate what their work rewards them with. This is quite different from how we used to think as children, before we learned about money. As ignorant children who didn't care about the cash and simply wanted to do great things, we wanted to have fun while being helpful. I doubt you said as a kid, "I want to work on Wall Street so I can make a ton of money!"

As kids, we liked animals and wanted to help them, so our dream was to become a veterinarian. We wanted to be a police officer or firefighter to save lives and help people. We didn't even know what money was, but when that changed, so did we. The aspiring pediatrician who wanted to heal children became a plastic surgeon, the wannabe vet started a slaughterhouse, and the kid who wanted to be a firefighter decided to become a defense lawyer instead. It's easy to see how these changes occurred when viewing success through the eyes of the world. Who's more successful? Is it the devious casino owner who cheats on his taxes and lives in a mansion, or a video rental clerk renting a small apartment and eating canned beans so he can do what he loves by writing movie scripts? Turn on the TV and the answer is clear. But who is really successful?

Even parents sometimes encourage their own children to seek out a future that pays better versus doing something they love. I don't believe they're trying to sabotage a potential happy future for their children; they just want what's best for their kids and believe that money is the answer. They have these beliefs because their parents had these beliefs and told them the same things. Either they considered themselves poor and felt that money was a form of security, or they were viewed as "well off"; either terrified to be without money, or without being able to picture life with less.

Some parents say, "Why struggle to become an Olympian when you could be a banker and own a big home? Don't be an underpaid photographer, get involved with a good company and work your way up the corporate ladder." While they may have good motives, these caring parents are ruining their children's dreams and altering their future for the worse. They subconsciously try changing their kids into who they want them to be, who the parents themselves wish they could have been, or who they think will best benefit the child down the road, usually in a financial way.

I believe these good-hearted parental figures never took the time in their own lives to determine what they wanted, and instead, let life choose it for them. A good way to know if this is the case is by looking at how they view work. If they think of work as an obligation rather than a choice, they haven't chosen what they truly wanted.

Have you been taught that money equals happiness and been convincing yourself and others of that same belief? Do you really have this belief, or was it (consciously or subconsciously) told to you? Have you ever stopped to ask?

Money has contributed a great deal to the kind of unwritten rules we've learned while growing up which have influenced our decisions since birth. Not only is it possible, but probable that these rules have distorted your true driver and what you find worth your time and effort.

I believe people usually have good intentions. However, I also believe that we have a tendency of putting our own needs and desires before the wants of others. While our parents, family, and good friends all want us to be happy, most people could care less. Some people only want what's best for them and understand how our decisions will consequentially affect their lives. They know that what we choose for ourselves can benefit them or make their situation worse in a number of ways.

Let's pretend that when you were a kid you wanted to become the President of the United States. Another classmate also wants to be the president, so he discourages you from having that goal. He knows that if you also ran for president, he would need to work harder, and that more competition equals more work. You can look at every aspect of life and realize how each individual's decisions will impact a number of other people. These influences can create illusory goals and persuade you to give effort toward things you don't genuinely value.

A common goal for many people today is making more money. If you make 70K per year, work hard, and receive a promotion to making 80K, that's great! You are now making $10,000 more every year. But was this goal your true desire, or was this an illusory goal?

Since you're the only one getting the pay raise, how will others be affected by this grand promotion? Well, our government will get paid on your behalf, and your employers can justifiably expect more from you. Assuming you don't spend every penny of the raise on yourself; your family and friends will get newer and nicer things. You may spend a portion of the money dining out, freeing time for your wife who would otherwise cook; plus, the restaurant owner's wallet gets fatter, and the server appreciates the tip.

Maybe you do spend the raise on yourself by purchasing a new sports car. Making an extra grand each month, you go to the bank and get a loan for the car. The bank benefits from the loan's interest, the car company gets paid, the car salesperson gets a cut, the oil companies benefit, and Uncle Sam gets a piece of it all. You also win, sort of, as you not only have a happier family or a new car, but also a better image in the eyes of all the people you've profited. They now treat you better, so you feel better about yourself. But while everyone benefited, only you put forth the time and effort to earn the promotion.

Let's say your driver was to become a military soldier like your father. Your dad, however, died in combat, and your mother doesn't want to fear losing you as well. She could easily discourage you from pursuing this dream in order to give herself a sense of security. She could even be doing so without realizing why, convincing you both it's for the better.

You could have a dream to move away and start a new life elsewhere. Could you be discouraged by your friends and family who may be concerned for your wellbeing or miss your company at home? Do you think your friends and family may miss you and try to discourage your move for their own selfish desires?

When truly giving it thought, every decision you make can and will impact a number of people in some way. By understanding this, you can clearly see how you may have adopted an illusory goal. Think of your driver and how it may affect others. Will it disappoint someone? Will it assist someone in pursuing their own dream? Could it cause you to lose friends, relationships, status, money, or self-image?

You'll most likely have to lose something in order to gain what you truly find worth doing. You can only put so much air into a tire before it becomes over inflated and useless. Picture your life as that tire. It can only hold so much, and in order to get some fresh air in, you'll need to let some out. How will you get the old air out? In other words, what can you afford to let go of, have less of, or eliminate?

David J. Gross

How Others Should Affect Your Dreams

We all have the desire for affection and community with others. We are also born with empathy and want others to be happy. However, to spend life trying to please everyone is futile. While politicians try, they prove the point that it's impossible. Most of us have accepted that disappointing people is inevitable, groups, religions, businesses, and even those closest to us. Fitting in with one crowd excludes you from another, to accept one religion rejects others, to shop at one store neglects giving business to another, and the list goes on. So, in acknowledging this, how should others affect what we pursue?

It's valuable to categorize each person into one of two groups, then pursue whatever we as individuals deem to be worthwhile so long as it does not compromise our integrity. The smaller and potentially non-existent group consists of people who rely on you for their wellbeing. The second group is everyone else.

The group who relies on you will consist primarily of your children, spouse, or people you take care of in some way. All these people who depend on you must be involved when considering a life altering decision. By getting on the same page and having their support, you will continue transforming your dream into reality.

Sometimes we make decisions that disappoint those we love, and this doesn't feel good. We have the most empathy for these people, and the idea of letting them down can be difficult. But sometimes it's necessary, for if we continually try pleasing our friends and family, we can end up disappointing ourselves. This can cause deep-seeded resentment and hinder an otherwise positive relationship. So, if there is a situation you cannot detach from without damaging your integrity, you must surrender to that situation and be at peace with your choice.

However, most situations can be altered for the better with communication and hard work.

Discussing an idea, desire, dream, or feeling that may disappoint those closest to you is an unnerving thought, but to quote Dr. Seuss, "Be who you are and say what you feel, because those who mind don't matter and those who matter don't mind." In other words, the people who care about you want you to be happy, and as long as you're not doing something illegal or immoral, they will most likely be supportive. It may take hours of thinking, discussing, and planning, but once you've convinced yourself of your passion, it won't be hard convincing others as well.

It's wise to be careful about revealing your dreams to others. Individual dreams and life pursuits are personal and fragile. Think of your legacy need as a fragile piece of art you've spent months, if not years, creating. You keep it locked in a secured safe and only you can access it. Being one of your most prized possessions, you would want to be very careful of who you let see and hold this delicate piece of art. The more people who hold it, the greater chance it could be damaged or destroyed entirely. So be very careful who you share your dreams with, and only do so with a clear reason in mind.

The goal is to get your fine piece of art out of the safe and onto display; turn your dream into reality. While you don't want to show your artwork to just anyone, especially someone who may be careless with it, it can be beneficial and many times necessary to share that masterpiece with someone who may be able to help. It's rare to have a dream that doesn't require the involvement of other people for it to become true. My dream was to move to Maui. While I did share this dream with some people who treated it carelessly, I also told people who greatly helped.

David J. Gross

If you reveal your passion to others, expect to hear an opinion, and if you pull your sculpture out of the safe to show someone, expect it to be affected in some way. Ideally, we would be able to hear the opinions, both negative and positive, and not be affected in any way. While encouragement and motivation can lift us up, negativity can easily bring us down.

In conclusion, your environment contains many people who are affected by your decisions. You may not even realize how many or to what degree, so be careful with whom you share your deepest desires. While many people will share their opinions with your happiness in mind, many people will subconsciously determine how their personal lives will be affected and then respond accordingly.

Observe Your Environment

- The only element of our environment we have the potential to totally control is our mind
- Our mind is not us, it is just one part of us
- Our mind wants us to feel good without feeling uncomfortable
- Being aware of all options brings celebration to the choices we make
- Life can feel like a mandatory obligation when constantly dwelling on the completion of daily events
- Success is seeking goals we as individuals decide are worth pursuing
- Before wanting better, you must know what better looks like
- Money can buy two things: time and comforts

    *A comfort is anything other than basic survival needs

- Illusory goals can persuade us into putting effort toward temporary things we don't truly value

- Every decision you make impacts a number of other people in many ways

- Not pursuing your dream because of others can cause problems in those relationships

- If encouragement influences you positively, discouragement will most certainly do the opposite

- Be deliberate with whom you choose to share your dream

P. Plan With Purpose

Plan (v.)- to arrange a method or scheme beforehand for any work, enterprise, or proceeding

Learn How You Learn

Once you've taken the first three actions of stopping everything, thinking about your past, and observing your environment, it's time to plan. Planning, like everything else in life, takes time. It also takes thought, patience, diligence, and motivation, so we first need to know who we are and what makes us tick.

After uncovering your dream, I would love to say to jump right into the goal-planning, positive thinking, and hard work, but I can't. Why? Because we've already tried that method and it didn't work. We've all read the books and heard the speakers tell us to think of our goals, write them down, and get motivated to go out and seize the day. They've told us to draw an outline and go over a step by step method toward success, but they never discussed the term itself.

A motivational speaker pumped us up to feel invincible; like we could conquer the world. A book showed us the path to success, giving us steps and ambitions and plans for achieving greatness; then something happened. We closed the book, left the auditorium, and had one of life's tragic misfortunes get in the way of our dreams. We lost focus and became so discouraged that we gave up and quit trying. We failed, but we shouldn't feel guilty. We wanted to get rich, lose weight, treat people better, be more active, and we got started with all the motivation in the world and then stopped. I believe we stop pursuing goals because we get started on the wrong foot.

First, we could have been pursuing an illusory goal and wanted what others wanted us to want. If we were indeed seeking our own dream, it's possible we believed the doubts, concerns, and discouragement from friends and family, and stopped due to fearing failure. Another reason people fail to reach their goals is by not taking the time to learn. We can't envision the task, effort, or reward because we don't first do our homework. We never learn enough about what we were trying to accomplish, but more importantly, we never learn how we best learn.

Learning how we individually learn was not taught in school or instructed by our parents. It isn't required to graduate, and most people go through life without ever giving it thought. Learning was required in school and has been necessary for nearly every job we've ever had. We can learn through all kinds of methods yet learning primarily remains (in both our private and professional lives) limited to just a few traditional methods. Maybe you had no problem reading a chapter from a book then writing a report. Perhaps looking at flashcards or taking notes from textbooks worked fine for you. If that's the case, keep it up. Don't fix something that isn't broken. However, if you're someone like me who has a hard time sitting still for long periods of time and isn't too fond of reading textbooks, it's time for something new. If you can't focus on studying by looking down at paper (especially at 8:00 A.M.), take some time to learn how you learn.

In school, we've all been taught the same material, the same way, and at the same time. The United States educates its children through set and regulated standard methods of teaching. Unless you went to a private school with an unusual schedule, school started around 8:00 in the morning, lunch was between 11:00 or 12:00, and around 3:00 in the afternoon you were dismissed. This is how life was structured from the time you were five years old, all the way through high school. Your time was scheduled and enforced through a signal, usually a sounding bell. If you missed the bell you were penalized, and if you were late multiple times you would have to stay after school in detention. If that didn't teach you a lesson, you were suspended and had to stay home (a punishment I never quite understood).

Not only were you told when you were taught, but how you were taught. Depending on your teacher, you may have watched movies, listened to lectures, been required to take notes, read silently, or read aloud as a class. For every teacher it was different, and each one taught in whatever manner best suited them. Unfortunately, teachers are not paid to help you learn, but paid to teach, and if you can't adjust to their teaching style, too bad! Are the teachers to blame? I don't think so. How could any teacher help every single student learn when they have hundreds each year? Teachers teach; it's up to the student to learn.

There is a tremendous difference between learning and being taught. We can be taught by dozens of teachers, mentors, and tutors, but we can only learn by choosing to do so. This can be best achieved by catering to our own unique learning preferences. If teachers teach in the manner that best suits them, why should an individual not learn using the best methods for them specifically?

Learning isn't as easy as being taught, especially when teaching styles conflict with your learning preferences. Time of day also plays a big role in the learning process, yet in the twelve years of general education, this was dictated. Our physical environment was another factor, again something we had no control over, especially if you attended public school.

David J. Gross

Do you know when you learn the best, in what environment, and through which methods? Are you a morning person, or do you feel most alert later in the day? Do you like to read, watch videos, listen to lectures and do worksheets, or would you prefer to learn in other ways? Are there other ways?

Start asking questions, as learning is essential to conquering anything regardless of how much you already know on the subject. If you dive right into researching how to climb Mt. Everest, you'll dive too deep, too fast, and hit your head on the bottom of the pool. What I mean is, with today's technology, there's a lot of information (and misinformation) available, making research feel overwhelming. Being overwhelmed by too many options can cause frustration to the point of giving up before starting. There's simply too much information on every subject and too many options for learning to choose from. There are too many websites to visit, books and articles to read, people to talk to, stuff to buy, films to watch, and places to see.

Learning can be a thrilling experience if we do it right, but if your high school was anything like mine, you had a history teacher who could care less about anything other than names and dates, and a lifeless math teacher who knowingly taught useless formulas and equations. Your classrooms were lit by headache-inducing florescent lights, and the wall air conditioning units barely worked. You studied outdated textbooks with fans blowing on your face while your science teacher used the same syllabus she's used for fifteen years. Forcing your way through crowded halls in a race to beat the bell, you spent time in physical education getting soaked in sweat. You then spent the last three hours of your day wearing damp boxer shorts only to arrive in English class to get a bad grade from using an apostrophe instead of a hyphen. Learning, as shown by our public-school systems, is anything but fun and entertaining.

From Mainland to Maui

A lot of us with similar experiences have adopted the belief that obtaining knowledge is uncomfortable, boring, irrelevant, and pointless because of these experiences. Our schools have done us a disservice by hiding the fact that knowledge can spawn imagination which can later develop into infinite possibilities of how wonderful life can be.

How do you prefer to learn? Think outside the box (school system methods) and ask yourself in what environments you learn the best. When using your mind, do you prefer sitting, standing, lying down, or exercising? Does your brain feel most active in the morning, night, or afternoon? Does drinking coffee or chewing gum help you focus? Do you thrive by having deadlines, or do you become self-motivated through having as much time to spend on a project as you wish? Have you ever taken the time to ask these questions?

If you're having trouble thinking of fun ways to learn, it could be that this is the first time you've given it thought. Don't be discouraged. Just meditate on ways you might learn differently with passion. The possibilities are endless if you have an active imagination.

Let's look at an example; pretend your goal is to become a cruise ship director. You like to travel and think the job of the director would be a wonderful goal to pursue. However, you have no clue as to what the job entails or how you could become educated on the subject. This is a unique goal which will take some creative thinking, for you can't go to college and sign up for a class on how to become a cruise ship director. In having unique goals, you need to think of unique ways of learning about them.

What are some unique ways to learn about this example? You could start by writing letters to every cruise line expressing your interest and requesting information directly. If they can't tell you much, see if you could send a letter to the directors themselves asking for a response or a phone call about how to get started. You could utilize the internet to find a cruise ship director, currently working or retired, who could provide insight. People love talking about themselves, so take advantage and gain some knowledge. You'd be surprised at how people are so willing to talk about their lives when given the chance. After getting a response, you may discover you need five years of cruise ship experience before being eligible for the position. You may also be told you need experience in public speaking and community organization, in addition to expansive boating knowledge. By learning what it takes, you've divided the main goal (learning everything you can about the position) into smaller goals (learning about boats, getting a job on a cruise ship, public speaking, etc.). In learning a few of the requirements, you've made the dream more real by having specific actions to pursue the goal. Success!

Looking at one of these more specific goals, how could you learn about working on a cruise ship? You could try to contact someone who's done it. Through friends, social events, work, and the internet, you could easily talk with someone who's worked in this multi-billion-dollar industry. With this being a more common position, there may even be books on the topic. Perhaps you could take a cruise as a passenger and gain information on board. The cruise lines could provide information on how to go about working for them, so writing a letter or visiting their websites could obviously be helpful.

Moving on to public speaking, you probably can't go to a school or church and request to get in front of the group to practice. However, you may have a friend in charge of a fundraiser where you could volunteer to speak at a rally of some kind. You could easily practice a speech by yourself in front of the mirror, or just rehearse a script for friends and family. You could become involved in your local community and volunteer to speak wherever you could gain experience.

From Mainland to Maui

To learn about boats, you could read books, talk to boat owners, watch videos, go to boat stores, or visit harbors to ask questions. You could take boat trips, volunteer to help clean boats in exchange for knowledge, or even buy a boat. There are dozens of ways to go about learning in unconventional, perhaps more appealing ways if you don't limit yourself to how you were taught growing up.

The plan when preparing to accomplish a goal is to know so much about it that you can mentally act it out. Not just day dream about it, but really imagine yourself going through the motions minute by minute in detail. In order to do this, you need to learn a lot. Be patient, remembering that taking the time to discover how you learn is success. Simply preparing to act is taking action in itself; and our legacy lies in our efforts, not just the results.

Knowledge Is Power

After determining the best ways, places, and times for you to learn, begin inhaling as much knowledge as your mind can hold. Time seems to always be against us. Do you agree? We need time to do anything, and most people don't have extra hours in the day they're seeking to fill. It will be challenging to free the time needed to learn and will take sacrifice. Not having ample time, or feeling as if you don't, can prevent any goal from thriving. You may have already learned a great deal about whatever you're pursuing. While this is a good start, unless you can visualize every aspect in detail, you need to learn more. You need to know so much about what it is you'll be attempting that you can lucidly act it out in your mind.

Remember what times, methods, and environments you learn best in, and always work around those preferences. Learn in the best way you can and stay motivated by reminding yourself that your dream is one of the most important things in life. It's more meaningful than owning nicer things (unless that is your goal) or watching sporting events. If you agree that setting out to achieve greatness is important, treat it that way! Give your dreams the best chance to become a reality by having time and knowledge, along with a willingness to alter routine and make sacrifices.

If you discover you learn best in the morning, learn in the morning. Let's pretend this was the case and you work a standard nine to five job. Your mornings are currently filled with a routine; showering, shaving, brushing your teeth, drinking coffee, eating breakfast, and driving to work. How could you free up some time every morning to learn without going to work hungry or dirty? Could you listen to an educational program on your way to work? Could you use the bus or railway, giving you the opportunity to read or write during the commute? Could you talk on the phone to a mentor while driving? How about waking up earlier? While it may take some getting used to, instead of watching an hour of TV at night, go to bed an hour earlier and spend the extra hour in the morning to learn. While late night talk shows can be entertaining, they have no lasting benefit. I'm not saying that to watch an hour of TV is a waste of time and serves no purpose. Sometimes an hour of TV is exactly what we need in order to help other aspects of life. I'm just saying that the hour to learn about your dream should be your first priority. If it isn't the first, it can easily become the last, and never given the time needed to survive.

You'll most likely need to get less of something to reap the benefits of having more time. Your life is a tire that can't remain effective while being over inflated. When having the option to be mindlessly entertained or use our brains, we'll usually choose the entertainment. Remember, our minds want to please us now by giving and receiving immediate sensual gratification. So, treat learning about your goal as if it were required for survival. View it as a need which, if not met, will cause conflict and regret.

Learning is just like lifting weights. When you first start lifting, you have poor technique and struggle with each repetition, only to wake up sore the next morning. The first few lifting sessions are uncomfortable, and all you can think about is what you'd rather be doing. After a couple of weeks of achy muscles, you start improving. You no longer wake up sore, the weights begin to feel lighter, and your technique improves. Exercising becomes easier due to the consistency and repetition. If you take a couple weeks off, the weights will feel heavier and you'll again wake up sore. Learning, just like lifting weights, becomes easier the more you do it.

While working toward your goal, always remember you'll be rewarded through patience and persistence. If you accept learning as a need, determine what schedule, or lack of, works best for you. If you're like me, you'll want to set aside specific periods of time to fully concentrate your attention. Then again, you may learn more easily in other ways. You may pursue your goal at spontaneous times throughout the day or sporadically throughout the year, taking weeks at a time to pursue your dream. Let your learning time work around your own preferences and how you learn the best.

It will be very easy to become impatient during this learning period. Reading an instruction manual is boring. It may even get to the point where learning feels like just another chore in your already busy life but continue reminding yourself that just by learning you're already achieving success. Success is not solely obtained by the finish line and how quickly we get there, but by having fun throughout the journey. In taking the time to learn about that which you find worth doing, you are being more successful than any millionaire who mindlessly goes through life in a comfortable fashion. Success is in trying, although that's not what our society tells us or how our dictionary defines the word.

In addition to misinterpreting success, our society has also done a great job of confusing stupidity with ignorance. Admitting ignorance can be an extremely uncomfortable thing to do. In school, by raising your hand to ask a question, you risk looking "stupid" in the eyes of your classmates. In reality, the only stupid people are the ones who either don't care to learn, have knowledge and choose not to use it, or who pretend they have knowledge when they don't. Ingrain this in your mind; it's ok to be ignorant. In fact, to admit ignorance is one of the smartest things you can do! Without proclaiming this potentially uncomfortable fact, no one would learn anything. We would all walk around holding our heads high pretending we're smart while truly just acting stupid. It's not easy, but if you can proudly proclaim to the world that you don't know what you're talking about or what you're doing, information will fall into your lap.

Ignorance can feel embarrassing, and our minds want to shield us from discomfort. Being ignorant can make us feel uneasy, and our minds do not like these negative feelings. It always wants to feel good, and embarrassingly admitting ignorance contradicts this objective. Some people prefer to remain ignorant for the sake of protecting their image, but these people will die without ever trying anything new.

Let's pretend you want to become a professional baseball player. You could run to the batting cages and practice without learning what it takes. If you wanted to become a ballerina, you could also ignore this advice and just dance. But at the batting cages you'll miss the ball, and while practicing ballet you'll fall. You're going to be discouraged. That's why learning is so important; it eliminates doubt. You'll likely encounter doubt in many forms from all sorts of outside factors and inside voices, and the last thing you need is more reason to believe your dreams are unachievable.

Another benefit to learning so much is being able to look at the worst-case scenario. This is something I've found to be extremely useful, for if you can accept the possibility of the worst result occurring, there is nothing to fear. The unknown is scary. In the dark, you don't know what's around, so anything could harm you. Chances are that you would be more afraid in the dark than if you were to actually see danger in the light. At least then you could see the potential threat. People daydream about doing extraordinary things yet never try because they can't see what the outcomes could realistically be, both good and bad. It's avoided because it's unknown, and the unknown is frightening.

If your goal was to start and grow a small business, what's the worst-case scenario? Let's say you've saved money for years, penny pinching everywhere possible so that one day you could start your very own dog grooming business. The absolute worst case I can perceive is failing miserably and the business going under in a matter of months. After saving money, quitting your job, starting your business and losing your investment, you're broke! While certainly an unfortunate series of events, would that really be so bad?

If you decided the effort to start the business wasn't worth the risk of failing, what could have been? You could have ignored your dreams and spent the money dining out more often, driving a nicer car and buying more expensive shampoo, but even if the business failed at least you could say you tried. You could keep a business card with your name on it; proof that you owned and operated a business. How many people can say that? Is that not something to be proud of, regardless of the outcome?

If the business did fail miserably, was anything gained? I have a hard time believing the business owner wouldn't have learned a lot through those years of pursuing his goal. He would probably have learned a great deal about himself through saving money, pet grooming, and the many tasks that go into a small business. I like how Thomas Edison responded when asked about his 1,000 "failures" while attempting to invent the incandescent light bulb. He said that he never failed, but rather found 1,000 ways not to make a light bulb.

So, what's your goal and what's the worst case scenario? If you get in your car and drive down the street, the worst scenario would be getting in a fatal accident or becoming paralyzed. Keep that in mind when trying something different. The most disappointing outcome couldn't be worse than that.

Make a Plan

Planning is the last and final step of preparation before getting started on your goal. You understand how you've been mentally limited and conditioned to think a certain way. You see how through years of schooling and societal influence you've been programmed to live within boundaries. You've learned about yourself, understand the roles of others in your pursuits, and know so much about your goal that you can taste it. The time has come to make a plan.

Consider your heart and soul (where your dream originated) as the owner of a team. This team is everything that comprises your being. Your appearance, attitude, mind, body, and self-image all go into "Team Real". As an owner preparing to put forth the best effort, you need to hire a good coach. You need to employ your mind.

The mind affects everything in life and is the basis of our environment. The way you think affects how patient and persistent you can remain when life becomes hectic and exhausting. Your mindset can prevent you from trying new things or encourage you to press on when times get tough. Our outlook on life influences experiences, goals, dreams and everything else, and will affect every area of your life for better or worse. Due to the importance of understanding this, I'll repeat: how you think, what you think, and the speed at which you think will always affect everything. So, as the owner of "Team Real", hire a good coach and get your mind set to a winning attitude.

The success of any team begins with the owner having a clear vision and positive coach who can execute solid game plans for success. Your mindset will need to take the role as a coach to remain confident through disappointments, keep you motivated when losing, and full of energy when you tire. You're a player in the game of life, with fans rooting for you and others cheering for your loss, and your mind is what makes the difference when the game gets seemingly out of control. When a game gets chaotic, good players stay calm. It starts with the coaching.

With a winning mentality, make plans naturally by using the same method used to learn. Customize where, when, and how you take action. Perform when you're most awake, active, and motivated. This again may need some schedule rearranging and creative thinking, for unique goals require unique plans.

Write down your plans and always be assured that what you're working toward is of the utmost importance. The pursuit of personal goals enables us to live instead of merely surviving. It's also one of the only things that separates us from animals who do nothing more than eat, drink, and breed.

Know yourself and make a plan to win. If your mind remains continually confident with a clear and focused game plan, the owner's happy, you will work hard, and the fans will rally behind you. In other words, your heart will be satisfied in pursuing your legacy, and your self-image will improve. With a plan to achieve something you know in your heart is worth your time and effort, success is inevitable.

Plan with Purpose

- Be successful by taking the time to learn how you learn

- Before seeking to fulfill your dream, learn enough to be able to mentally act it out

- Not having ample time, or feeling as if you don't, can hinder the development of any dream

- Merely having money in the bank and nicer toys makes no one a success

- Admitting ignorance is one of the smartest things you can do

- Knowledge counters doubt

- Accepting the worst-case scenario can eliminate fear

- How you think, what you think, and the speed at which you think will always affect everything

- Live successfully by rejoicing in the choices you make and the legacies they create!

From Mainland to Maui

While appearing easy on paper, slowing down to understand what you value, freeing time to try something extraordinary, and having the courage to admit ignorance are some of the most difficult things in all of life. I wish you luck in whatever you choose to pursue and hope you take to heart the contents of this book by patiently accepting that the most important thing is starting on the right path; your path. Ask yourself questions, dare to admit ignorance, and challenge the way you've been living. Discover what it takes to fulfill your legacy needs and strive for greatness.

Knowing who you are will lead to passion. Pursuing these passions is success. Enjoying our success, we may spend every moment in peace. We can be joyful, appreciative, feel alive, and spend every minute doing exactly what we want. Each day will be filled with purpose, and we will live rejoicing in our choices and the legacies they create.

Aloha,
David

www.ingramcontent.com/pod-product-compliance
Lightning Source LLC
Chambersburg PA
CBHW061943070426
42450CB00007BA/1035